JUMP
ATTACK

THE FORMULA FOR EXPLOSIVE ATHLETIC PERFORMANCE,

TIM S. GROVER

WITH SHARI LESSER WENK

Souvenir Press

To every athlete with a dream

and the relentless desire

to achieve it

CONTENTS

ACKNOWLEDGMENTS

Sincere gratitude to all who contributed to this project: my agent and coauthor, Shari Lesser Wenk; everyone at Scribner, especially Shannon Welch and John Glynn; and photographer Jim Forni and his talented crew at Octane Rich Media.

Most important, this book would not exist without the legendary athletes who have trusted the power of this program and believe in me as much as I believe in them. Their unstoppable drive for greatness is proof that no matter how good you are, you can always be better.

JUMP
ATTACK

CHAPTER 1

TAKING FLIGHT

N ear the end of Michael Jordan's career with the Bulls, he agreed to allow a camera crew to follow him around for a documentary on his last season in Chicago.

Early one morning—it was still dark outside and Michael's kids were still asleep—the crew came to his house for a rare glimpse into his private gym where I trained him.

The complete video has never been released, but I can tell you how it began:

The cameraman noticed a poster on the wall, a classic shot of MJ soaring through the air, with the caption "HOW DOES MICHAEL FLY?" He zoomed in on the poster, then turned the camera to Michael and asked him:

"How *do* you fly?"

Michael just laughed, shook his head, pointed across the gym at me, and said in that deep, commanding voice, "Ask him."

Good question.

No doubt Michael's genetics gave him a physical advantage; he has those huge hands and long limbs and predominantly fast-twitch muscles that allow him to do extraordinary things. But contrary to popular legend, he is not a freak of nature. I know people mean it as a compliment when they talk about Michael as if he's superhuman.

But I see it as an insult, because it suggests he didn't have to work for his success, and believe me, no one ever worked harder.

In fact, there are plenty of athletes who share his physical abilities, and in some cases even exceed them. But Michael had the mental toughness to exceed anyone else's physical abilities, along with the drive and commitment to work relentlessly on his skills, and that toughness is ultimately what separates merely great athletes from iconic superstars. That's why Kobe Bryant and Dwyane Wade, in their thirties, can outplay guys who are much younger; like Michael, they have the mentality and focus and work ethic to maximize their skills, push beyond injuries, and never stop driving to improve.

So there are undoubtedly a lot of factors that allowed Michael to fly. But when he pointed at me in his gym that morning, this is what he meant: We trained in a way that maximized his abilities and gifts and genetics, so he could reach his ultimate potential in every way, and still keep improving. We tweaked the standard training principles, because there was nothing standard about Michael's game. While everyone else was still obsessed with vertical jumps, we focused instead on overall explosiveness. Not just one jump straight into the air, but multiple jumps in all directions, forward, backward, laterally, and maintaining that explosiveness throughout the entire game, from one end of the court to the other.

Everyone loves the showstopper dunk, but what happens right after that dunk? The game doesn't stop; neither did he. We trained for longevity and overall athleticism that would allow him to stay healthy and powerful from the opening game of the season until he held the championship trophy in June, season after season.

And that training—the "secret" to Michael's explosiveness and his ability to take flight—became the basis for Jump Attack.

The first version of this book was created in 1990, when Michael was doing a lot of camps and clinics and everyone kept asking him, "How do you jump so high? How do you dunk like that? What can I do to increase my vertical jump?" Everyone wanted to "be like Mike," so he asked me to put together something he could give to everyone who attended, a program they could do on their own that reflected the hard work he put into his own body, so everyone could see he didn't just show up and look good—he worked relentlessly to be that good.

I developed the original Jump Attack program based on the workout I created for him, which was completely different from the way anyone else was training. At that time, no one else was doing resistance training for the legs during the season; the common belief was that playing basketball and running up and down the court were enough. In fact, it was just the opposite; playing a sport actually breaks down the muscle. So we went the other way and worked on building up the muscles that have a tendency to break down over the course of a long season.

We also began sequencing his exercises to get the most out of every muscle, every time. We focused on preexhausting the targeted muscle, loosening the joints, combining exercises to teach the muscles how to fire correctly, stretching the muscles and joints immediately after so they'd be ready for the next set.

While most programs were targeting the major muscle groups, we were also emphasizing the smaller muscles, the neutralizers and stabilizers, so everything was working together.

And we definitely got people talking when they heard MJ was lifting on game days, which was basically unheard of at that time but made perfect sense to us. Look at the schedule: If you take off every game day, that's a whole lot of days you're not working those muscles properly. For us, not acceptable. So we stayed with our workout schedule regardless of the game schedule. It became part of his game preparation; just like you eat a certain way on game day, you train a certain way on game day.

Bottom line: You can't get extraordinary results from an ordinary workout.

And if you're thinking, "Sure, it worked for MJ, how hard can it be to make MJ look good?" think again. It was quite a challenge to take someone like Michael Jordan, who already had superior ability, and make him even more superior. My challenge: If he's this explosive, if he can jump this high, how can I make him even more explosive? How can we get him to jump even higher?

When you're dealing with the greats—and I've been fortunate to train many—the room for improvement is so small that we're constantly looking for the slightest edge, the tiniest detail or adjustment that will give them the advantage. So Michael's workout program was designed with that in mind: Build on his greatness and make him unstoppable.

Yet it was clear to me that even though the program was created for the best of the best, it would work for anyone, not just the greats. So I expanded the workout into a book, called it *Jump Attack*, and self-published it. Over the next few years, I sold hundreds of thousands of books through mail order, filling out address labels and carrying packages to the post office. When Michael retired, I figured that was that. We sold out, and I didn't print more.

Then one day I got an email from a young basketball player saying he found the book on eBay for $1,000. That is not a typo. One thousand dollars. I started looking around, and found there were more like it, selling for hundreds of dollars all over the Internet. Before long I started getting emails and tweets from athletes and coaches and parents asking how they could get the book.

I realized that even though science and research and training had evolved since we released the original *Jump Attack* more than twenty years ago, I was still using the same core concepts with my clients, and they were still getting the same explosive results and increased athleticism. The only difference was now we had ways of getting those results faster and more effectively. All these years later, the same training principles still form the foundation of what I do. From Michael Jordan to Kobe Bryant to Dwyane Wade and so many others, this works.

I also realized it was time for an entirely new book. Now we know so much more about elite training, how to train all the muscle groups so everything works together, how the body responds to rest and recovery, how nutrition affects performance, when to stretch and how to stretch. We know how to condition the central nervous system to create faster reflex action and faster explosive contractions, so you don't have to think about what you're supposed to do, your body just knows. By tweaking the exercises in small ways—something as simple as elevating your heels or changing the leg position of a lunge, for example—we can attack the small muscles that most programs completely ignore. I enhanced the program to work all the different muscular contractions—isometric, concentric, eccentric—as we work through every phase of developing explosiveness. I also added upper body and core work designed to make the entire body more explosive, not just the legs. I changed the exercises and schedule to keep it fresh and challenging. The result is an entirely new workout: the all-new Jump Attack.

The core concept of the book remains the same—we're still using the exclusive sequences I use with every one of my pro athletes—but the entire program has been updated to give you state-of-the-art training for unprecedented results. If you're one of the hundreds of thousands of athletes who worked out with the original

Jump Attack, you will discover that this program contains entirely new exercises and challenges. If you've never tried this program at all, believe me, you are about to experience something completely unique, train like you've never trained before, and see improvements you probably thought were impossible.

Jump Attack is a total-body workout—lower body, upper body, and the entire core—that delivers measureable improvement. From the world's greatest athletes to the kids just starting out, everyone has room to improve. In fact, the greats *have* to keep improving, because they know someone is always coming up behind them, trying to knock them off the top of the mountain. So it's never an option to stay in the same place, feeling good about what they've done, content to be where they are. It should be no different for you; no matter what level you're at, you can always go higher, and this program will take you there. It's not easy. But if you want proof that this program works, just ask any of my clients; everyone who works with me trains with some version of this workout.

I'm going to ask of you the same thing I ask of all my clients: Do the program exactly as I'm giving it to you and give your maximum effort.

That's it. If you can do those two things, here's what you'll get in return:

- Explosive athleticism for improved performance
- Increased vertical jump, muscle mass, power, speed, and agility
- A tighter, leaner physique
- Mental toughness and endurance
- Effective rest and recovery
- Nutritional guidelines for improved performance

- Injury prevention
- Improvement in your overall ability

Jump Attack works because it takes challenging moves, combines them in a specific order to maximize results, and tests your ability to push yourself to new levels. This is not a weight training program; the goal is not to see how much you can lift. The goal is to train your muscles for maximum explosive force. If you want a bodybuilding program for beach muscles, look elsewhere. You'll definitely develop muscle tone, but we're going for overall athleticism, not just great biceps. And it's not a weight loss program: You might drop weight if you have weight to lose, but that's a by-product of the workout, not the goal. I don't want skinny athletes, I want strong, explosive athletes. You might actually put on weight as you put on muscle. I expect you to eat like an athlete so you can build the muscles you're going to need to perform at your maximum ability in any sport or activity.

This is a program designed for athletes who are committed to seeing how high they can go, and are willing to make the commitment to find out. Are you ready to get serious about your body, and discover what you're capable of achieving? Are you comfortable being uncomfortable? If you're serious, if you're ready to change your body and your game, if you're committed to showing up and doing the work, you're on a journey that will set you apart from the competition and take you places you never imagined.

It works. This is how my pros do it. If you want to become more explosive, stronger, and faster, if you want to jump higher and improve your overall athletic performance in any sport, this is exactly how we do it today: the difference between jumping and taking flight.

This is how the best get better—and you will too.

CHAPTER 2

THE RELENTLESS PURSUIT OF EXPLOSIVENESS

The first question I'm always asked about Jump Attack: "If I do this workout, will I be able to dunk?" I can tell you this: You will be closer. If your only goal is to dunk, you can get there with this program, but I want you to do so much more. And you will.

Increasing vertical jump and explosiveness is one of the most difficult things to accomplish in athletic training; it requires specific muscles to be activated and firing for a prolonged period of time. If you're doing it correctly, everything works together for extraordinary results; the right training will send you soaring over the competition. The wrong training will leave you flat on your feet.

When I started working with Michael in 1989, his vertical jump was 38 inches. At 38 inches he was already at the top of the game, and his dunking ability was not in question. So part of our goal with this program was to take him even higher, just to see how far we could get. We were going for increased explosiveness in every area, not just an increased vertical, but the vertical was definitely a by-product of the training. We got him up to 42 inches, and eventually to 48 inches before he took a break from the NBA in 1993 to play baseball.

Ten inches over several years, for the greatest player in the game.

Now, if you're hoping this program will add ten inches (or more) to your vertical jump during this ninety-day program, let me just tell you up front: That may not happen.

I know there are thousands of books and DVDs and programs promising massive increases in your vertical jump. I understand that the vertical jump stat is a great number to brag about and an easy way to compare yourself to others.

But it's just a number. And it's definitely not the only number if you're serious about athletic performance. Everyone gets so caught up in the numbers at the big scouting combines, waiting to see how much athletes can bench or how fast they can run the 40 or how they do on the vertical jump.

None of that gives an accurate measurement of how an athlete can actually perform in a game.

This may surprise you, but I don't measure my players' vertical jumps. If a team or agent or player wants that measurement I'll get it, but the answer is irrelevant to me.

Why? Because the ability to jump straight up one time or jump onto a tall, immobile object is not a way of predicting whether you can do that repeatedly during a game. It doesn't make you a better player or allow you to perform in an unpredictable or unstable situation. Vertical jump is meaningless if that's all you can do; jumping higher doesn't mean you will perform better overall, and dunking doesn't translate into being a better athlete. I've had players who could barely dunk a ball but could run faster and last longer than anyone else on the team. Who has more value, the guy who can jump high one time, or the guy who can keep going until the last second on the clock? The ultimate test is what you do during the game.

No sport requires you to stand in one place and jump straight up one time. Even if you're going for a jump ball or a block, you still have to perform countless other moves during a game; that one vertical jump isn't going to allow you to excel at everything else. Why focus only on that number?

An increased vertical jump is definitely a by-product of this program. But it's not the overall goal. I'm not training you to take a test. I'm training you to be an explosive athlete.

Think of it this way: You can prepare for a test and pass it if you have a few good study tricks and some basic facts nailed down. But if you don't really understand what you studied or how to use what you learned, you'll never be able to apply the information in real life. Do you go to a doctor just because he did well on his exams, or because he can practice medicine? I want you to test well *and* apply what you learned.

I'm not saying there's no reason to measure your vertical jump; if it helps you to see your gains, then go ahead and measure. You'll actually be able to test yourself twice during this program; I included it here because I know most people want to take the test as a measurement of their results. It's good bragging rights if you improve. But don't make the mistake of thinking an increased vertical jump is the only way to improve. I hear people say they went from 23 inches to 26 inches and they're disappointed. Then I ask if their ability has improved, and they realize how much they've actually achieved. Use the measurement as a guideline, not as a "score" or a test you can pass or fail.

The true art of athletic jumping isn't just about going up, it's about how you come down, hit the floor, and shoot back up again.

Effective training enables you to jump repetitively, getting into position for the next jump, and performing at peak levels for the entire game. You need to be firing those muscles over and over, from different positions, under different conditions, with opponents in your face. One jump under controlled conditions in the gym has nothing to do with game time performance. I train athletes for real life, not one number on a chart.

I don't care how high you can jump for a quick measurement. I care if you can jump while you're running. Can you explode off one foot? How about two feet? Can you jump while falling backward? Can you explode laterally? Jump Attack will give you the ability to do all of that. We're going for total explosiveness and repetitive jumping in every direction, in any situation, so you can—and will—excel in your performance throughout the game. Not just once but over and over.

I would love to tell you that if you do this program, you will achieve unlimited results, but unfortunately, that's probably not true. Everyone—and I mean everyone—has physical limits. The simple truth is that we all have different genetics and a different level of athleticism and different potential to excel at different things, and it's up to you to determine what you can do, and not dwell on what you can't. You may not jump like Michael Jordan, but he might not bench press like you.

Whatever limits you may have, this program will help you stretch them and get the most out of your abilities. You can—and will—show improvement if you do this program correctly. You might see progress in your vertical jump, your one-step jump, your running jump; you might become quicker or stronger or faster. Something is going to happen for you. Some people are more disposed to move quickly, some will jump higher, some will be better runners, some will move better laterally. Some people get quick gains and then plateau, others might see all the improvement at the end. That's almost always a result of genetics, not determination. True for the pros, true for you.

Everyone will get a different result from this program. You'll see an overall improvement in all areas, but you'll probably experience a remarkable improvement in one specific area, maybe in a way you didn't even intend, an unexpected by-product of your workout, determined by how you're built and how your body moves. For example: I worked with a guy who was one of the most explosive players in the league, had an unreal vertical jump, and he wanted to increase it even more. While working on that, he realized he had also developed his ability to move from side to side, backward and forward, making him a tremendous defensive player. Not what he had intended, but this workout had dramatically increased the flexibility in his hips, giving him not only the results he wanted but so much more.

If you do the program correctly and you complete the whole schedule, here's how you'll get the best measurement of your results: Use your new athleticism to perform in real game situations. I don't care how high you can jump in the gym. I want to see how you play the game. Measure your success by how this program makes you an all-around athlete in your sport. Maybe your vertical went up "only" 4 inches and that disappoints you (which it shouldn't). But when you're playing, pay attention to how much quicker you can get down the court or the field. How fast can you get around your opponent? How's your second jump? Are you finishing shots you weren't able to finish before? How much faster can you explode off the line? We're measuring results by your stronger legs and tougher body. When your opponent can no longer get that rebound in the fourth quarter, when he's too fatigued to play defense, when everyone else is gassed and you're still feeling good . . . that's how you measure the success of this program. Don't get caught up in meaningless numbers. Can you do something now that you couldn't do before? Are you playing defense better, are you quicker laterally, are you getting height on your second and third jump? Yes? Congratulations; you've succeeded.

There are numerous reasons Jump Attack gets results like nothing else. I don't want to throw all the science at you, but I think if you understand how it works, you'll have greater success as you go through the program.

Jump Attack works because it takes all the elements of elite training and combines them, like carefully measured components of a formula. There's nothing secret about any of the components; when you look at them individually, they're all easy to understand. But the science—and the unparalleled success of this program—is in how we combine them: the order of the exercises, how they're paired with other exercises, the duration of the sets, the speed of the reps, the muscles we preexhaust and stretch, the structure of the phases. The formula is based on how it all comes together.

Look at it this way: You can buy a can of Coke and read about all the ingredients on the label. You can go out and get all the ingredients, and spend years trying to figure out how to put them all together. But we both know you're not replicating that can of Coke. Why?

You don't have the formula.

You can take apart a Big Mac, go buy the meat, buns, tomatoes, lettuce, cheese . . . but the secret is in the special sauce, and without the formula, you can't create that sauce. You'll have an ordinary burger. No formula, no Big Mac.

In this book, I'm giving you the formula for excellence. I'm giving you the formula for explosive athleticism. Not just the ingredients, but the ninety-day step-by-step instructions for combining them. Any program can give you squats, lunges, tuck jumps . . . okay, you have the ingredients. So does everyone else. Do you know what to do with them so you can be *better* than everyone else? The details, the order, the pairing of the exercises, how to create the different types of muscular contractions, the number and speed of the reps? That's what Jump Attack gives you: the formula for putting it all together so you can train and succeed like no one else.

Keep in mind that this formula was originally designed for the best of the best, and has been used by countless elite athletes over the past two decades, with proven and incomparable results. So I've had a long time to observe and study those results, to determine what works and what works even better. I've had many years to hone and craft and tinker with the formula as science and our knowledge evolve; I can't imagine the results we would have had twenty years ago—with Michael and Scottie and Olajuwon and Barkley and so many others—using the science we use now to train Kobe and Dwyane and all the rest of my clients. And believe me, every player I've worked with from then until now has had an impact on this book. As much as they learn from me, I learn from them. Everything here is based on time-tested performance and results.

Since the program was first developed in 1990, there have obviously been changes and advancements in fitness and training, which is why the workout in this book is different from the original Jump Attack. Science has shown us new ways to activate certain muscles, identify the areas that have a greater tendency to tighten up, effectively loosen up those areas before, during, and after the workout, and enhance the ability to become more explosive. So over the years

I've integrated the new science and advancements into the program. The result is that you have everything you need to take it to a new level — using all the smaller muscles, not just the obvious big ones, working in phases to prepare the body for what's coming next, adding details to the exercises so you're working in ways you've never experienced. We're not just lifting weights, we're lifting them from different angles, and combining weights with intense plyometrics so your muscles can learn what they're training for. We're not just going through a bunch of exercises, we're doing them in a specific order and adding preexhaustion moves and stretches to make sure every muscle gives maximum effort. We're training those muscles by lengthening and shortening them so they can snap like a rubber band to give you that explosive response every time you want it. And we're combining all of that with intense core training, because it's not just the legs that give you flight, it's motion of the entire body, everything working together for maximum results.

You don't get extraordinary results by doing the same ordinary program everyone else is doing. Everything about this workout is different from anything else you've ever done. This is the difference between where you are and where you want to be. Give yourself ninety days to commit to excellence and give maximum effort, and I will give you results and improvement using the same proven formula I give my pros.

CHAPTER 3

THE JUMP ATTACK FORMULA FOR FLIGHT

O bviously, the best way to understand how Jump Attack works is to do the program and experience it for yourself; you can speculate about how the burger will taste, but you can't know for sure until you actually taste it. The more you can learn about all the ingredients, the better you will understand the formula and its unmatched results.

STICK TO THE SCHEDULE

I can't stress this enough: Follow the program exactly as I'm giving it to you. Science is about precision; you must strive for 100 percent accuracy in your work to get accurate results. The same goes for fundamentals of this program: If you mess with the formula, you will compromise your results.

Everything is designed to give your body the opportunity to achieve maximum results. There's a reason certain exercises are done before others, for a certain amount of reps or time. I know there will be times you'll want to do more, when you'll want to get ahead of the schedule or do extra reps or weight. Don't. You'll be cheating yourself, because your muscles may not be ready for the challenge, and that will actually slow your progress.

SEQUENCE THE EXERCISES

Every workout in this program is based on my Explosive Sequences, comprised of exercises that must be done in a specific order. There are fifteen unique sequences in this book, five in each phase of the workout.

Each sequence has three parts:

- a preexhaustion move to fatigue certain muscles and to loosen the hip area;
- a combination of different muscular contractions and plyometrics;
- a stretch.

As you'll see below, each part of the sequence is a critical part of the formula for explosiveness. Take out any part of the sequence, and it becomes just another workout.

Fact: If you do the sequences out of order, if you blow off the opening move, if you think you don't need the stretch . . . you are not going to get the results you want.

Everything you do prepares you for what's next. We're working in three phases, to take your body through the correct progression of growth and development. Phase 1 prepares your body for flight; Phase 2 teaches you to take off into the air; Phase 3 trains you to land and take off again. By the time you get to the most challenging moves of the program, your muscles will be ready to work at an extreme level of athleticism, conditioned to handle the force and impact. For example, my Attack Depth Jumps involve ten rapid jumps from a variety of heights and positions that train you to move quickly from jump to jump. Most programs put depth jumps in the beginning of the schedule, because everyone thinks that's the fastest way to increase height. But if you do these moves too soon, you can't get the maximum results because your muscles aren't ready; they haven't yet learned what they're supposed to do, and instead of jumping with strength and skill, you end up flopping all over without control of your body and you'll probably get injured. It's one thing to jump up, but there's an art and science to landing, absorbing the impact, and springing back into the air.

Here's more on the elements of sequencing.

PREEXHAUST THE MUSCLES

When you want to target certain muscles, you can get better results by isolating those muscles first by preexhausting them, so they have to work even harder during the exercises that follow. For example, it's very hard to work the glute muscles for explosiveness, so we're going to spend extra time working those first so they can get the same results as the other muscles we're training. By preexhausting the glutes, the primary muscles—quads and hamstrings—will work even harder during the exercises, and the preexhausted glutes will be working to full capacity. That's why every sequence begins with an exercise that isolates the muscles in the glutes: You'll be doing a lot of Fire Hydrants, Glute Bridges, and a combination of the two. I can't emphasize enough the importance of doing these to get maximum results; I want *all* your muscles working. There may be times you'll get to that move and think, "I did that already!" Yes, you did. So what? Do it again. These moves were designed for great results. Want the results? Follow the formula.

LOOSEN THE HIPS

At some point during this program, as you're doing your billionth set of Fire Hydrants, you're going to ask (or probably groan) "Why?"

Plain and simple: You loosen your hips and strengthen your glutes to increase athleticism.

There's obviously a lot of jumping in this workout, and the more you jump, the tighter your hip flexors become. And it's not just from jumping; running will have the same effect, as will sitting at a desk all day or being told by your coaches to get low into a crouch . . . that tightens the hip flexors as well. Tightness creates friction, and friction slows you down. The tighter the hips, the less athletic you become. So we're working to reverse that, over and over, to keep you loose and flexible. I don't need you so flexible you can do the splits, but flexible enough to be functional and effective while playing your sport. Muscle and joint stiffness do not benefit you in any way.

We're going to train those muscles to snap like a rubber band. Tight muscles give you a short little snap. Longer, looser muscles give you the long and effective snap you need to be explosive.

So do all the moves, do the stretches, no matter how many times they appear in the workout.

COMBINE EXERCISES FOR
MAXIMUM EXPLOSIVENESS

Almost every sequence in the program combines two specific exercises—one using weights, one using jumps—that have been paired for specific results. If you did the exercises separately and randomly, you'd still get a workout. But you won't get the explosive results this program delivers when you do them together.

For example: Just about every training program includes some kind of squat. You can do squats until you're the greatest squatter in the gym, but what's the end result? You've taught your body to squat. Not at all what we're working for here. We need to teach your new powerful muscles that you're training for a specific result. So we do those squats, then immediately follow them with a plyometric exercise, so the muscles learn what they're supposed to do.

In this program, you're training to launch your body in all directions, over and over. You're training to bounce. Imagine you're throwing a rubber ball in the air. When it lands, does it thud against the ground and sit there? No; it immediately springs back up. The higher you throw it, the higher it bounces back up when it hits the floor.

That's why we pair certain exercises, and work them in sequences: we're teaching your muscles to launch you into the air and land and launch again, making you jump like that ball, training your muscles for fast, repetitive action and developing the springs to allow you to bounce back up. Remember, if you're only training to increase your vertical, you'll end up jumping high and landing hard. No bounce, no action. Thud.

We're getting rid of the thud.

Most programs don't train you to do that. They train you for that one max jump, and that's it. What's the point of that? You've jumped once, you've landed. Then what? You haven't trained your muscles to repeat the action, so you're done. But real-life sports is about the whole game, not just one moment, and that means training your body to absorb the impact when you land, and applying more force into the floor so you can spring back up. *That* is the art of jumping, the ability to hit the ground and soar back into the air.

ENGAGE EVERY MUSCLE GROUP

I'm asked all the time: Which muscle has the biggest impact on jumping?

Let me answer this way: Which jump has the biggest impact on your game?

You can't just choose one. You need all the bricks to build a house.

Think about it. Do you jump the same way every time, from the same angle and position? Of course not. Each jump is a different situation, and each situation requires different muscles. So we're training them all to work together.

Back in the seventies and eighties, the common wisdom was that jumping was all about the calves. By the nineties, everyone decided it was the quads that made the difference. Eventually it was the glutes and hips that got all the attention.

Well, guess what? If you're emphasizing one group over another, you're going to have a physical imbalance and a weakness in your performance, and it's very likely that you'll get injured. All the muscle groups are equally important, not just in your legs but in your entire body; everything works together. If you've only trained your quads, all your jumps are coming off one muscle group. But add glutes, hamstrings, and calves, and now you're using four major muscle groups instead of one. Imagine how much stronger and effective and explosive you'll be when you get everything working together, so you can jump off one leg, two legs, from any angle. Jump Attack gets all the different muscles working at all the different angles, so you'll be explosive whether your knee is bent at 90 degrees, 110 degrees, 40 degrees . . . it won't matter. We're training you for every possibility, no matter how your hips and knees and ankles are positioned, so you don't have to think about it. I don't want you to think; I want your body so well conditioned that you can move by instinct.

SNAP THE RUBBER BAND

Some programs claim you don't need weights, or you only need weights, or you don't need plyometrics, or you only need plyometrics . . . ridiculous. You need it all. And here's why:

Training for explosiveness requires you to elongate the muscles so they stretch and snap like a rubber band, over and over. A short rubber band will give you a short snap; a long rubber band snaps harder and with more intensity. The more you can lengthen those muscles, the more explosive you're going to be.

But you also need the strength that goes along with that snap, which means we also have to shorten the muscles with heavy lifting; you need the heavy lifting to overload the muscles. If you *only* lift heavy, you end up stronger but slower, without the elasticity needed to snap that rubber band.

This is the only program that trains you by shortening *and* lengthening your muscles at the same time. In Jump Attack, you'll be doing three types of work: eccentric, concentric, and isometric. Eccentric contractions (which lengthen the muscles) are the most difficult, which is why they're in every phase of this program. Concentric contractions (which shorten the muscles) are the easiest, which is why they're the basis for most other programs. Isometric contractions look the easiest, but believe me, looks are deceiving (you'll understand what I mean when you finish Phase 1).

This is why you can't be successful in this program if you don't do all the phases or you skip around or you don't stick to the schedule. Without all the components of the formula, you can't develop the explosiveness that's going to send you soaring.

THE TRUTH ABOUT STATIC STRETCHING

As you'll see, each of the Jump Attack sequences includes a static stretch, where you get in one position and hold it to elongate the muscle. Ask any number of trainers about static stretching and you'll get any number of responses about its benefits or hazards; some say it decreases athletic ability or slows down your progress.

Let me set the record straight on this: Static stretching is an essential part of this program, and every one of my clients does it. The way you'll do these stretches in this program prepares your muscles for the next challenge; they will not slow you down or affect your performance, because we're stretching very specific muscles for a specific reason: to make the exercises more effective.

Most people stretch the muscle they've just worked; it feels good, because static stretching has an anesthetic effect on the muscle. That's exactly why we don't always want to stretch those muscles we're working; who wants to anesthetize a muscle you're still training? Over the years, we learned it was more effective to stretch the surrounding muscles that were most likely to tighten up and prevent you from getting an effective workout; in this case, the hip muscles, because we're using them over and over, and they have a tendency to shorten and tighten. We want to keep them lengthened, and the best way to lengthen those muscles is through static stretching.

That's why every leg workout in this book includes a stretch for the hip flexors. We use the hip flexors so much in this program that they have a tendency to tighten up, which can cause the hips and back to get thrown out of alignment. If we can keep them loose and stretched all the time, it allows them to fire better so you'll have a more effective workout.

It's important that you do the stretches every time they appear in the workout, and do them completely, because you'll be sacrificing and compromising the rest of your workout if you don't.

REST AND RECOVERY

Many programs have you do weights and plyo on separate days, several times a week. But we do them on the same day, so you're overloading the muscles only twice a week. Why? Because I want you to put maximum effort and intensity into those two days, and you can't do that if your muscles are fatigued from too much work.

Everyone thinks weight training builds muscle. That is false. Weight training actually tears down muscle. Your body then repairs and builds new muscle during your recovery, especially while you sleep. You cannot effectively build muscle without that recovery time.

When you're working on explosiveness, your recovery time is as important as—if not more important than—the training program itself. They go together. You cannot get maximum effort and results out of tired muscles. If you're overtraining, you're going to get weaker results than a person who undertrains. If you think sneaking in an extra day of lifting is going to speed your progress, let me assure you, you're doing the opposite. If you think you'll get better results by doing the sequences three times a week instead of twice (as prescribed), you are incorrect. In fact, if you did the sequences only once, you'd have better results than if you did them three times. Why? Because this program is extremely taxing, and you need complete rest to be ready for the next workout. For example, you'll do heavy legwork on Day 1 and Day 4, which gives you enough time to recover between workouts. I don't want you doing more legwork than that. Rest, recover, and take care of your body.

And during your workouts, I also want you resting between sets, because this program is for maximum output, it's not a race to see how fast you can finish. Your muscles need adequate recovery so they can give you the best opportunity to get your best results. Think about the guy who runs sprints; he's not going to race twice immediately back-to-back with maximum effort, he's going to take time to rest and recover between heats to give his body time to prepare for the next challenge. That's how I want you to approach your workout. I'm not talking about taking fifteen minutes to make phone calls and grab a sandwich, but listen to your body, know how much time it needs to prepare for the next set, and give it what it needs so it can give you the best results.

YOUR ANIMAL INSTINCTS

Fact: Humans are not designed to jump or fly.

Becoming explosive in any sport is actually one of the most difficult things to do. It's harder than losing weight, harder than getting in shape. Why? Because humans are built to walk, not jump. You have to train the body to jump. Natural for many animals, not for humans.

Note I said *train* the body, not *teach* the body. What's the difference? Training conditions your body to move instinctively. Teaching forces you to stop and think about what to do. Training is for action, teaching is for thinking. I don't want you to think; I want you to act from instinct.

Ask any little kid to jump, and he jumps. And he jumps and jumps and jumps all over the place because he can. He doesn't stop to think about how to jump, he just knows. He may not jump very high or with any great skill, but his body knows what to do. Then ask an adult to jump. He stops, thinks about it, and says, "Why?" He can't remember the last time he jumped, and decides he probably can't do it. Thinking, not acting.

Animals don't think before they act.

This workout will condition your body to know what to do, to move naturally, so you don't have to think about it. We're training the muscles to be ready when you are, so you can explode in every direction under any condition. That's it. I want you so well conditioned that your body is ready to take you wherever you want to go.

SWEAT THE DETAILS

When it comes to excellence in training, the slightest details make all the difference. Something as minor as turning up the toes on a certain move, landing so your hips are above your knees, where your hands are positioned—all of those little details that most people don't pay attention to are carefully built into this program so you can keep the pressure and impact where they're supposed to be. Remember, when I designed this program for Michael, he was already the best, and he was training to become better. You don't get there by doing sloppy work or doing the same work as everyone else, you get there by paying attention to every detail. That's also how you increase longevity, building your body and skills to stay strong and healthy. We're not training you to have one great season or one great game; this is training for a lifetime of greatness.

CHAPTER 4

RULES FOR RELENTLESS TRAINING

E veryone wants to know the secrets.

What's the secret to jumping higher?

What's the secret to putting on muscle?

What's the secret to faster recovery?

What's the secret to being the best?

No question, the Jump Attack program reveals the answers to a lot of those "secrets." If you're reading this book, you already know the secret isn't about taking shortcuts or sticking to the same old routines that didn't work before. Athletic success is the result of knowing what to do, the willingness to do it, and the drive to continually improve at it. I don't care how much natural ability you have, if you don't use it correctly and constantly work to elevate your talent into actual skill, you cannot and will not improve or succeed. All the "secrets" in the universe can't help you if you're not willing to push yourself harder than ever before, and trust that this workout will take you where you want to be.

But there's one more part to the formula, and you can't succeed without it.

You want to know the #1 secret for success in sports, or in anything you do?

Mental toughness.

The truth: 90 percent of what you do physically is controlled by what you do mentally. Your mind tells the body what to do, not the other way around. Decide. Commit. Act. Succeed. Repeat. In that order. The first two steps start in your mind, the rest turn into physical results.

In 2013 I wrote a book called *Relentless: From Good to Great to Unstoppable*, all about mental toughness and dominance. The book describes the "Relentless 13," the traits of the most intense competitors imaginable, a group I call "Cleaners." Cleaners are driven to succeed, and they know how to get results, whether they're athletes or CEOs or teachers; they get it done and move onto the next challenge. Anyone can be a Cleaner if you have the right mind-set and you're willing to commit to excellence.

That book was about being relentless in your life, and this book is about being relentless in your training. And since this book is exclusively for and about athletes, I'm going to give you a new list, for the Cleaner athletes out there, those of you who want results and are willing to work for them. These are my Rules for Relentless Training, and none of them involves how much weight to lift or what kind of shoes to wear. This is all about getting stronger from the neck up, so you can take on the challenge of getting stronger from the neck down.

As you'll see, all my lists are labeled #1 because when most people see a numbered list, they think #1 is the most important, #2 is slightly less important, and #10 is almost an afterthought. On my lists, everything is equally important, so they're all #1.

RULES FOR RELENTLESS TRAINING

1. Show up, work hard, and listen.

I don't care how much you can lift, how fast you can run, how many pull-ups you can do, or whether you can hit a three while blindfolded. There are only three things I ask of every client, and I'm asking the same of you: Show up, work hard, and listen. That's it. It requires no talent, no special genetics, or any skill whatsoever to show up, work hard, and listen. Just walking in the door, you're already ahead of most people who give up or won't even take the first step.

Back when I trained MJ, the last thing I said to him after every game, win or lose, was "Five, six, or seven?"

Meaning: What time are we working out tomorrow morning?

He'd throw back a time, and that was it. No discussion. At whatever time he agreed to, he showed up, he worked relentlessly hard, and he listened both to me and to his body, because he knew everything we were doing was part of the plan to get that end result. That's not about skill, it's about the commitment to excel.

While you're using this book, showing up means sticking to the schedule, being ready to work, and doing exactly what the program asks of you that day. Working hard means giving your maximum effort for maximum results, no shortcuts; if you find yourself thinking "good enough," it wasn't. And listening means paying attention to detail, following the directions in this book exactly as I'm giving them to you, looking closely at the photos to make sure you're doing everything right. It also means listening to your body, because you're the only one who will know if you're shortchanging yourself by not doing enough work, or setting yourself back by doing too much.

I don't care if you're the best guy on the team or the last guy off the bench, your willingness to show up, work hard, and listen says more about you than you can imagine. After a loss, after a rough game, when your body is aching from a tough workout, when you have personal problems . . . showing up says you have the mental grit to move forward, that you're prepared to improve and you're able to set aside distractions and negativity. That is the sign of an extraordinary leader.

1. You don't have to love the work, you just have to crave the results.

I get calls from athletes and agents and GMs in every sport, at every level, asking for help with conditioning, training, performance. We spend some time talking, I listen to their concerns and goals, and I devise a plan that will get them where they want to be. You'd be surprised by how many guys come in, hear the plan . . . their eyes roll back in their heads and they say, "Ummm . . . too much, good-bye." They want to play but they don't want to do the work. And in most cases, they're saying good-bye to their careers shortly after.

If you don't crave that end result, if you don't want it more than you've ever wanted anything, you'll never make the mental commitment to do the physical work. Training is hard; excellence is harder. You don't have to love it. You just have to believe it's worth it in the end.

Guys such as Michael and Kobe and Dwyane were born with extraordinary ability, but they know the truth: It's not enough to get to the top. You have to fight to stay there. Sometimes when I'm training Kobe, he'll stop for a moment, glare at me, and say, "What we got left?" I tell him, and we get back to work. We always get back to work . . . because he craves the end result.

Do the work because you want to do it, because you have the healthy body and opportunity to do it, not because you *have* to do it. People always say you have to "love" what you do. I disagree. You have to love the end result. You have to be addicted to the greatness of finally getting what you worked for, no matter how hard and tedious the work was. Ultimately it's the work that makes the end result so much sweeter.

1. Get comfortable being uncomfortable.

Everything you do in the gym becomes easier when you stop expecting it to be easy.

If you're thinking about how hard it is, how much you're sweating, how many minutes are left on the clock, how you can't wait for it to be over, you'll never get through a serious workout. Go into your workouts knowing they'll be tough and tiring. If you're doing it right, you're putting your body through something incredibly taxing and challenging. Why else why would you be doing it? Get the fear and dread out of the way before you start. Accept that it's going to be hard, you'll recover when it's over, and you'll come back for more.

You have to show up and do what's required of you every single day, regardless of whether you feel 100 percent. You're not always going to show up feeling great, so get rid of those expectations, because you still have to do the job. A pro always feels great on the first day of his career and the last day of his career. On the first day, he hasn't done anything yet and his body feels healthy, his mind is clear and hopeful. On the last day . . . he finally gets to exhale. No more pressure, no more work, no more ice baths or therapies or Advil. As MJ said to me the day he retired, "If I ever see you in my neighborhood again, I'm going to shoot you." It's over. Suddenly everything feels better.

Any program that tries to sell you on getting results in ten minutes a day isn't a workout, it's an insult. If that's all you've ever done, I guess it's better than nothing, but is that really what you're working for? Better than nothing? Training is about taking your body places it's never gone, putting it through new experiences. How else *should* you feel? If you feel the same, if it's all comfortable, doesn't that mean you're not doing enough? When your needle hits the uncomfortable zone, that's when you know you're doing something right. I'm not talking about pain. I'm talking about that moment when you know you've pushed your body to its limits and accomplished something incredibly challenging. Was it uncomfortable? Probably. Was it worth it? Absolutely.

1. Anyone can start something; very few people can finish.

How many times have you started a workout program, made a resolution, vowed to stay with it, gave it everything you had . . . and within a week, you already quit. Just like all the people who start working out the first week of January: The gym is packed, everyone has their big dreams for the new year, and they make the ridiculous commitment to be there three hours every day. Never in their lives have they worked out for three hours a day, but once a year, they try out the idea because it sounds good.

Then they get hurt, pull a muscle, tear something, because they're not prepared for that kind of workout. Or maybe they just get busy. Can't make time to do all that work. Don't want to make time. Whatever the case, it's February 1, and the gym is a lot less crowded than it was a month ago. They've all given up.

It's not just you. I see it with the pros all the time. They show up the first day ready to go, crush it for three hours. Day two, their lower body is sore and they haven't worked their upper body yet, so they spend another three hours on upper body work. Day three, the lactic acid is burning and they stop showing up because every muscle in their body is obliterated and they're not comfortable being uncomfortable.

I look for certain qualities and behaviors in an athlete to determine whether he's serious about training, but one of the most critical tests is whether he shows up that third day.

Take it in stages. You don't have to work out 24/7 to get results. In fact, that would be counterproductive. That's why Jump Attack is designed in phases that take you through the proper stages of developing explosive musculature without overworking your body and forcing you to quit. If you look at the first phase and think, "Too easy!" (because there is no jumping and almost no weights), do it anyway and then let me know if it was too easy. If you do it correctly, if you give it everything you've got, I promise it will be very challenging. And it will deliver results.

1. When everyone else is giving up, that's when you push yourself harder.

Even the pros get to a point in a workout when they just can't go any more, or there's an exercise they can't do. It happens to everyone. Some people say, "That's it, too hard." Others say, "Okay, let me get at this."

The first thing I ask is, "*Why* can't you do this?" Is there a physical problem? Are you injured or damaged in some way? If you are, you need to respect your limitations. Talk to a doctor. Heed his or her advice. But if it's not physical, that means it's mental. You've told yourself this can't be done, so now it can't be done.

The only thing that can push you past this barrier is your own mental toughness, your desire to keep going. Look, I understand sometimes that box you have to jump on looks like it's eight feet tall, and the weights you're holding feel like they each weigh a ton. If you can't do something because of physical limitation, you have to adjust. But otherwise, you should be able to do all the exercises in this program. If something is too challenging, rest briefly and continue. But no quitting—you're finishing every exercise even if you need rest as you go. If the sequence calls for a ninety-second hold, and you can do only forty-five seconds, take a brief rest and get back for the next forty-five seconds. If I ask you for fif-teen reps and you can give me seven, take a brief moment to recover, then give me the other eight. You want to train like a pro? This is how we do it. We finish what we start. However many breaks you need, take them and finish. Most people give up. Be the one who doesn't.

1. You play on two feet, you train on two feet.

Fact: Animal predators aren't slow or fat. Think about it; most creatures with killer instinct are fast, lean, agile, competitive. They have to move like lightning to catch their prey and dominate their surroundings. You have to move. If you're an athlete or serious about fitness, and your workout involves spending most of the time lying on your back or a bench or a ball while training, you need to fire your trainer immediately. Or if you're not using a trainer, you need to find one to show you what you're doing wrong. You compete on two feet, you move on two feet, you get everywhere using two feet . . . why the hell are you lying down to train?

Science is constantly giving us new information that helps us get better results using less time and energy. No question some of it has made training and recovery more effective and efficient, but there's still no replacement for hard work and sweat. I do a lot of work on athletes using muscle activation, which is basically a way to get the muscles to contract while the athlete is lying on a table in a horizon-tal position. For some athletes, this is a dream come true: Wait; you mean I can work those muscles but I can keep my butt on the table? Where do I sign up? They're all crushed when I tell them muscle activation is only one part of our work, and get off the damn table because we still have some real work to do.

And yes, I have lost clients over this. Somewhere, sometime, some trainer told these guys they could get great results with little effort on their part and they were like, "Sign me up!" Okay, good luck. Those are the guys I usually hear from later in the season, but now instead of sitting on the table they're sitting on the bench.

You don't need gadgets and gizmos and contraptions to be in good shape. Push-ups, pull-ups, squats, lunges, presses, walking, running. Back to the basics. Now there are machines for everything, and they're all designed to make the work easier and easier and easier. That's what people want, but it's not what they need.

Get moving. Get on your feet. Move your body. If you're not training like an athlete—sweating, breathing, physically driving yourself to exhaustion—how do you expect to play like one? How you train is how you play.

Even on rest days, when you're not working out, the worst thing you can do for tired, sore muscles is to lie around doing nothing and feeling slow. Get up—I'm not saying you need to run a marathon, but take a walk—and flush out the lactic acid, use the new muscles you've been developing. I promise, you will feel so much better once you're moving around.

1. Think "I want to" instead of "I have to."

Truth: You do not have to be here. You don't have to train, you don't have to work out, you don't have to spend one more minute pushing your body and mind to their limits. This is your life; you are free to go.

Or . . . you can choose to be here. Not because someone told you to, but because you want to, because you want to be challenged, because you have goals you must achieve. For yourself, not anyone else. "Have to" is always for someone else. "Want to" is just for you.

Wanting it is the first step to giving your maximum effort. It means you're not dragging your ass, thinking about where you'd rather be. You're here because you *want* to make the team, win the title, get the starting job. I've been around so many youth clinics where some parent or coach is screaming at the kids, "Come on! How bad do you want it?" Guess what? If the kids don't want it for themselves, they just don't want it.

This is about your body, your goals, your personal pursuit of excellence. Only you can decide how far to take it or how much it means to you.

1. Decide what you're willing to give up to have what you want.

What are you willing to give up? If you can't spend an hour without your phone, tweeting and texting, if you can't train without watching a big screen TV, you're not going to make it through this program, and you're definitely not going to make it as a serious athlete.

Every player in the NBA starts out as a kid trying to get to the top. The few who actually make it aren't always the best—believe me, there are guys out there playing ball at rec centers and parks who have the talent to play in the pros, but they never get there. Why? If the talent and skill are there, why aren't those enough to get you in the door?

Talent and skill will get you *to* the door. What happens

next is up to you, because walking *through* that door means you're leaving a lot behind, including your friends, free time, other activities. That door represents a commitment that few are willing to make, and even fewer are able to maintain. When everyone else is heading out for a night with friends, you're still in the gym. They're all sleeping in; you're up early so you can fit everything in your day. Practices at dawn, games late at night. If you get far enough up the ladder, you get endless bus rides and plane flights and schedules with zero flexibility. You'll miss birthdays and holidays and all sorts of events, all for this one commitment. Greatness comes with a price, but it's worth every penny if you're willing to pay it.

1. It's good to train hard, but better to also train smart.

Jump Attack isn't just about working out. We're working out for results. Not just getting through the exercises, but focusing on what you're supposed to do, striving for improvement and maximum effort. That means you're training smart, not just working hard.

I hear from so many young athletes who are frustrated because they don't think they're getting their chance. "I work hard," they say, "but nothing happens!" Well, are you working on the right things? Did you do a hundred push-ups with terrible form, or fifty push-ups with perfect form? Are you putting in time working on fundamentals, or did you spend your workout time on fancy dunks for an imaginary highlight reel? There are highlight players, and there are fundamental players. The highlight guys want to dunk but put no effort into the basics, and you cannot be exceptional without the basics. The truly great players can do both. They don't just wait for a big moment. They *create* that big moment by doing the little things. When they practice, they master basics over and over and over. Everyone wants to shoot threes in the gym, but training smart means you're working on your free throws as well. That's training smart, instead of just training hard with no specific plan or goal.

When someone tells me he worked out so hard he puked—and thinks I'll be impressed—all I can think is, Was that your goal? To get sick? That's not training smart. Even after you clean up and get back to work, you know you're not going to be able to give your maximum effort. You sabotaged your workout by forcing your body to train inefficiently.

The same goes for practicing at "game speed." Nothing wrong with that, how you practice is how you'll play. But "game speed" doesn't mean "full speed" for the entire practice. A real game changes speeds constantly: fast and furious, slow and controlled. It doesn't mean going crazy for an hour in practice; you'll fatigue faster and end up having a lousy practice. That's not training smart.

I hear from players all the time—even the pros—who say they can't put on weight. They work out constantly and eat around the clock, but they can't build their bodies. I'll always ask what they're doing to train and eat, but I already know the reasons: They're spending hours in the gym working on their shots but not lifting weights; they're eating loads of carbs to replace what they're burning up but not enough protein to build new muscle. So they stay lean and thin instead of adding muscle and bulk. That's training hard but not smart.

You know that if you train, eat, sleep, and work for

results, you'll probably get them. But knowing it isn't the same as *doing* it, and that's why most people never achieve those results. They "Yeah, but . . ." themselves out of the gym. "Yeah, but I can't do that." "Yeah, but I won't get to play anyway." "Yeah, but I don't have the time." "Yeah, but [fill in your own excuse]." When what you're doing isn't working, it's up to you to find out why, and then do it right.

That's training hard *and* smart.

1. Face failure head-on.

I don't believe in failure; failure is what happens when you lose trust in yourself, and you decide you've failed. As long as you keep working to get where you want to be, you haven't failed, you're adapting to a challenge that you can ultimately conquer. Ignore those who tell you otherwise; most people will knock you down and tell you what you can't do because it makes them feel better about their own failures. Refuse to absorb the negativity; no one can define your success or failure because you—and you alone—set the goals.

Even the greats have setbacks: injuries, losing seasons, poor performances. But true winners show up the next day ready to work, no matter what happened the day before. The measure of your success is how fast you work to turn things around, and how hard you're willing to work to achieve a better outcome.

1. Refuse to be satisfied, because there's always more to do.

You're truly content with what you've achieved? Congratulations on your accomplishments, you have officially stopped improving.

The minute you're satisfied, it's over. That relentless drive to do more, to go higher than anyone else, to be the best at what you do . . . you can only achieve those by never being content with where you are. Killer competitors never lose sight of that: Whatever they do, they want more. They don't want perfection because that means they can't improve, and they're obsessed with improving. They don't rest physically or mentally, because they're always thinking about how they could have done it better, faster, smoother, in some way no one else has ever done it. There's joy in getting the job done, but it always comes with the reminder that there's still more to do.

Why would you want to be like that? I'll give you one reason, and it's the same reason that explains why you're reading this book.

The reward is just so good.

CHAPTER 5

JUMP ATTACK Q & A

REQUIRED READING

Before you begin the program, it's essential that you read this section and understand the basic important instructions for being successful in Jump Attack.

Over the years I've been asked countless questions about this workout. Most of them can be answered with either: (a) "I don't know if you'll be able to dunk but you'll be closer," (b) "Yes, you have to do the squats," or (c) "Sorry, I can't take you to meet my clients."

But there are other, more pertinent questions, so before we get to the workout, let me address other common questions and concerns, to give a good idea of what's ahead for you as you begin the program.

HOW MUCH TIME WILL I NEED TO COMPLETE THE PROGRAM?

Jump Attack is a twelve-week program, divided into three phases; each phase prepares you for what's coming next. You'll do each phase for three weeks, then take a week to completely recover before beginning the next phase of the workout.

The schedule gives you four training days each week: two leg days and two upper body days. The other days are for rest and recovery; you will need them, and as I discuss in the chapter on rest and recovery, I expect you to use them.

Each workout should take you approximately an hour; it may take you slightly more time in the beginning and less time by the end. If the workouts are taking you much longer than seventy-five minutes, you may be working too slowly or taking extra-long breaks. We're working for speed and explosiveness, so keep going even when you feel like you've had enough. You will get there.

WHAT EQUIPMENT DO I NEED FOR THE WORKOUT?

Everything you need for this program can be found at your gym or health club or your school's weight room:

- Barbells and weights
- Dumbbells
- Bench
- Plyo box
- Clock, timer, or stopwatch

WHAT YOU DON'T NEED DURING THE WORKOUT:

- TV
- Video games
- Phone calls and texts
- Snack breaks

You're here to work; you can't give focused effort if you're distracted. You know how it goes: You go to check your phone, and suddenly there are three things you have to deal with right away. Ten minutes later, your muscles are cold, you're running out of time, and it's easier to just quit your workout for the day. For this one hour, make yourself the priority and make everyone else wait. Leave the entertainment and gadgets somewhere else. They'll still be there when you're done.

I DON'T WORK OUT AT A GYM. CAN I STILL DO THE WORKOUT IF I DON'T HAVE ALL THAT EQUIPMENT?

You can get some results without all the equipment, but if you want to see actual improvements, you need everything on the list. No way around it, no shortcuts. Real results require real dedication. A true craftsman needs his tools.

If you really don't have access to barbells and a rack of weights, you can use heavy dumbbells, but you will not achieve as much as you would with weights. The only way to become more explosive is to overload the muscles, and one of the most effective ways to overload the muscles is with weights. If you want results you have to train for results.

WHAT ARE EXPLOSIVE SEQUENCES?

The Explosive Sequences are the critical component of the legwork in Jump Attack. Each sequence includes:

- a preexhaustion move (to slightly fatigue the muscle, loosen the hips, and prepare your body for what you're about to do);
- a combination of isometric, plyometric, and weight exercises;
- a stretch.

There are five sequences in each leg workout—fifteen in the whole program—and you must do them all, in the correct order.

The Total Body workouts do not have sequences, but you still have to do the exercises in the correct order; most of the exercises are done in supersets.

IS THERE REALLY A DIFFERENCE BETWEEN EACH PHASE OF THE WORKOUT?

Each phase is completely different, designed to get you ready for what's ahead, preparing your body for more challenging work.

- Phase 1: Fire—isometric hold moves, for extended lengths of time. No weights or jumping. Looks easy. It's not.
- Phase 2: Force—more isometric hold moves immediately followed by weights, plus plyometrics. You'll hold a position, then explode into reps. We're teaching the muscles what they have to do, then making them do it. I'm not training you to be a world champion at lunges, I'm training you to do lunges so you can be more explosive. So we'll use the muscle, then put it to work so it becomes conditioned to performing athletically.

- Phase 3: Flight—timed weight exercises, plus plyometrics. We're training you for speed; let's see how fast you can move the weights and keep the muscles firing.

CAN I DO THIS PROGRAM IF I'VE NEVER WORKED OUT BEFORE?

The exercises in Jump Attack aren't complicated, but proper form is critical so that you don't become injured during the workout. This program is designed for athletes who have some experience with weights and understand the form and technique required to do the moves safely and for maximum results. If you are not familiar with the exercises in the program, ask for help from a knowledgeable trainer before attempting the workout. Follow the exercise descriptions and photos closely.

I'M RECOVERING FROM A SERIOUS INJURY AND NEED TO GET ACTIVE AGAIN. CAN I DO THIS WORKOUT TO HELP ME GET BACK IN SHAPE?

Jump Attack is not a rehab program. Before attempting this workout, consult with your doctor or licensed physical therapist to find out whether you're far enough along through rehab to begin this level of strenuous work.

DO I HAVE TO BE A CERTAIN AGE TO DO JUMP ATTACK?

This program is intended for ages fifteen and up. By that age, your body is ready to benefit from the weights we're going to use.

Athletes under fifteen can do Phase 1. I do not recommend the rest of this workout for athletes younger than fifteen, who have more growing to do; their bones aren't dense enough and the ligaments and tendons aren't strong enough. Younger athletes benefit the most from playing their sport, and doing exercises that require only their own body weight.

IS JUMP ATTACK ONLY FOR BASKETBALL PLAYERS?

Nope, this program will benefit any athlete in any sport. You'll be able to go from season to season and be explosive in whatever you're doing. A football lineman isn't jumping into the air, but he has to explode into action from a down position so he can push someone backward. A swimmer has to explode off the blocks. A baseball player has to explode down the baseline to steal. Hockey players explode into action when the puck drops. Think about a sprinter: Not only does he have to quickly jump forward out of the blocks, but he also immediately has to shift into a running movement. Everything in this workout is designed to make any athlete more explosive, training you to move in all different ways, using all the different muscles for maximum impact. But you have to teach the body what you want it to do, which is the purpose of the Explosive Sequences; we're not just doing squats, we're following the squats with plyometric jumping exercises. We're building a foundation to maximize explosive athleticism.

Each sport is different. That's why I want you playing your sport on rest days so you train your new muscles to adapt to your sport. The technical name for it is Specific Adaptation to Imposed Demands (SAID), which is a scientific way of saying the body will learn what you teach it. When you do this program and play basketball, you'll be explosive for the demands of that sport. Play a different sport, and you'll be explosive for that sport instead.

Remember when Michael Jordan went to play baseball in the middle of his NBA career? A couple of years before he decided to do that, he started asking me for a baseball workout. Here was a guy with the most incredible athleticism imaginable, yet even he knew he'd have to train completely differently to play a different sport. So we developed a workout for baseball, so his shoulder muscles could learn to throw a ball fast in a straight line, without the arc he needed for basketball. His legs had to learn that instead of jumping straight in the air to dunk, he'd have to explode forward down the base paths or across the outfield to catch a ball. And even though we were training for baseball and not basketball, we still used the Jump Attack program, because remember, this workout is for overall explosiveness, not just one jump straight up.

When he returned to the NBA, we used this program again to retrain those muscles; now he was explosive for baseball, but not basketball. His basic skills hadn't diminished, but the muscles had been working for a different result. Your body will adapt to whatever sport you're teaching it to play. When you train exclusively for one sport, you need to retrain and reeducate the muscles to perform a different sport. This is one of the reasons I like to see younger athletes play more than one sport; it keeps the body in balance and prevents athletes from overusing the same muscles.

When Michael came back shortly before the playoffs, I knew he wasn't yet in peak basketball condition, but we got him as close as we could in a short time. When the Bulls lost to Orlando in those playoffs, everyone said he wasn't the same MJ, that he had aged and declined.

We knew better. After an off-season of Jump Attack–style sequence training, he wasn't as good as before . . . he was better. And he returned that season to win the first of three more rings.

Jump Attack targets the specific muscles you need to make you more explosive in every way. Train the body to do what you want it to do, and it will give you what you want.

CAN I CHANGE THE ORDER OF THE SEQUENCES OR THE DAYS I'M SUPPOSED TO WORK OUT? CAN I SWITCH EXERCISES IF SOMETHING IS TOO HARD?

No, no, and no.

The program is the program. Everything is where it is for a reason. Each workout is based on my Explosive Sequences that must be done in the correct order to get the full effect of the workout. There may be parts you don't enjoy or you find particularly difficult. That's fine. If you can't do ten reps, do as many as you can, take a short break, and then do the rest. If you can't do perfect Tuck Jumps, I still want you to do the best Tuck Jumps you can do. Maybe you'll improve each time, but even if you don't, we're not skipping Tuck Jumps.

And if you do skip something or decide to change the program, know in advance that you're likely sacrificing your results.

This isn't a weight loss program where you can choose your own cardio and still burn calories. We're training your muscles to do something complex and specific, and that requires complex and specific work. Get comfortable being uncomfortable, and stop letting your body tell you what to do. If you're thinking about how hard it is, it just gets harder, so if you have to think about something, think about the results you're working for and how great you'll feel when you achieve them.

WHY DO SOME OF THE REPS AND TIMES DECREASE INSTEAD OF INCREASE THROUGHOUT THE PROGRAM?

I know it's contrary to the way you're used to training—in most programs, everything goes up—the reps, the times, the weights—because the stronger you are, the more you can do for a longer period of time. But as you probably know by now, this isn't a weight training program; we're working for a specific result that has nothing to do with how much weight you can lift. The challenge is to train the muscles to snap faster and faster, not lift heavier and heavier. So over the course of the three phases, as some requirements increase, others will decrease. You'll be asked to work either less time or do fewer reps, but you're going to continually increase the height you have to jump, or the amount of weight you're using to see how fast you can move that weight. As the program progresses, as you use heavier weights or increase the height of your jumps, I don't necessarily need you to do ten reps; you can get the desired effect in six reps. Instead of holding a position for thirty seconds, you can get the job done in twenty seconds. Sounds easier, but believe me, nothing we're doing here is about making it easier.

IS THERE A SPECIFIC WARM-UP ROUTINE FOR THIS PROGRAM?

I'm not giving you a specific warm-up routine; if you're ready to do Jump Attack, you should already know how to warm up your body.

Give yourself five to ten minutes to get your muscles and joints warm, and get your core temperature slightly elevated. Do a dynamic warm-up, jump rope, get on a stationary bike, do jumping jacks in all directions, stretch. Just warm up the body, loosen the joints, and make sure you're not working a cold muscle. The warm-up shouldn't be a workout; most programs put you through a lot of cardio and moves that go on for way too long. That's not necessary and can be counter-productive. Don't overthink it; just get warm.

Don't skip it. This program is demanding, and if your muscles aren't ready for the work, you could injure yourself. Staying healthy and injury-free are essential if you're going to succeed here. Think of a car on a cold morning: It's hard to start, and it takes a while to get the engine warm. If the engine gets too hot, you're going to be stranded on the side of the road. Take care of your body before the warning light comes on.

IF I'M ONLY WORKING ON MY EXPLOSIVENESS, WHY DO I HAVE TO DO THE TOTAL BODY DAYS?

Let me ask you this: Do your legs operate independently from the rest of your body? Do you play a sport that doesn't involve your arms or torso? If the answer to those questions is no, you're going to do the Total Body workout.

There's more to jumping than going straight into the air. Think of your body as a long spring that pulls apart and comes together, and to create maximum results, that spring has to work as one unit to explode into action. Whatever sport you play, it's about that first explosive moment of attack. Basketball, golf, volleyball, football, tennis, baseball . . . explode and attack. We're training the whole body to work as one unit. That includes the shoulders, arms, back, core (which includes every muscle from your chest to your knees), and every muscle in the legs.

If you already have an upper body program that you do for your team or yourself, you can stay with it or switch to this one, but don't do both; you will be overtrained. If you find that you don't have time to do both Total Body days, you can do only one day. But if you're in a sport that intensively involves your upper body—tennis, golf, baseball—do two days.

WHAT IF I DON'T HAVE TIME TO DO
THE WHOLE SCHEDULE EVERY WEEK?

The schedule gives you four workouts each week, two for legs and two for the upper body and core. Obviously I would like to see you do the entire schedule: Explosiveness isn't just about training your legs, it involves the entire body, and this workout is designed with that in mind. Four days a week really shouldn't be too much if you're serious about overall athletic improvement.

But I know that many athletes have to do other workouts for their coaches and teams, and you may have to adapt this program to fit in with your other requirements. If that's the case, here's how you can modify the Jump Attack schedule:

- At the minimum, do the two lower body workouts each week. You will definitely make progress, although if you do the entire program, you'll make a lot more progress.
- The Jump Attack schedule has lower body workouts on Day 1 and Day 4. If you have to adjust that, move Day 4

to Day 5 instead. *Do not* shorten the time between lower body workouts; I want you to have at least two days of recovery before you overload those muscles again.

- Make sure you're getting at least one upper body workout each week, using either the Jump Attack program or your own. It's essential that you continue to work the entire core — upper chest to just above the knees — so your whole body is working explosively.

I STARTED THE PROGRAM BUT THEN I STOPPED, AND I WANT TO GET GOING AGAIN. DO I HAVE TO START FROM THE BEGINNING?

It happens. Everyone goes through those times when they can't train, or they don't want to train, or something unexpected throws them off the routine. Don't let a brief interruption turn into a permanent vacation. If you're serious about working out, get back as soon as you can. The shorter the break, the faster you'll be back in gear.

If your Jump Attack schedule was interrupted, here's the schedule for jumping back in:

- If you missed a week or less, pick up where you left off.
- If you missed two weeks, repeat the last two weeks you did before you stopped, and continue.
- If you missed three or more weeks, start over.

CAN I DO THIS WORKOUT DURING MY SEASON, OR DO I HAVE TO WAIT FOR THE OFF-SEASON?

You absolutely can do Jump Attack and still play your sport. The pros do it every day: They go through practice, a stretching routine, maybe a game, and we build their strength and conditioning program into their schedule. You can do the same.

Here's how the program should fit into your schedule:

On Day 1 and Day 4 (the leg days), we need your legs to be fresh, so do Jump Attack first thing in the morning, before team training or practice or workouts. If you can't do it early and you have to do it later, then do it; I don't want you skipping a day just because your legs might not be completely fresh. I don't recommend doing this right after practice; give yourself a couple of hours to recover. The goal is to give maximum output, so the more rested you are, the better the results.

Same goes for the Total Body workouts on Day 2 and Day 5; schedule your workouts for when your upper body—shoulders, arms, chest, back, abs—will be the freshest. Give yourself the best chance to get the best results.

Ideally, this is a great off-season workout that lets you show up for the new season more athletic, explosive, ready to impress, and deliver results.

CAN I DO JUMP ATTACK ON A GAME DAY?

This is a strenuous and demanding program, so I would not recommend doing the workout on a game day; you will probably feel fatigued. However, if you usually work out in the morning before a game, your body will probably handle the challenge. Most of my athletes lift in the mornings, so their bodies are accustomed to it. By the time they go to shootaround and then the game, they're completely recovered and mentally prepared for what they're asking their bodies to do. People always say to me, "I can't believe they lift on game day . . ." Well, if your routine is to lift on game day, then you lift on game day. But if you don't want to do that, look at your schedule and start the program on a day that won't conflict with your games.

HOW CAN I DO THIS WORKOUT IN ADDITION TO MY TEAM WORKOUTS AND COACH'S PROGRAM?

First and foremost, you have to make intelligent choices about your training. If your coach has given you a workout routine, be careful combining that one with Jump Attack because overtraining is more detrimental than undertraining. Too much work equals less results. Your body won't recover enough and your muscles won't allow you to put the maximum amount of work into each workout that this requires. So if you think there's a conflict between your team program and this program, talk to your coach or team trainer, show them the workout, and work with them to see how to proceed. Honestly, I don't know a single credible program that doesn't include squats, lunges, dead lifts, and Bulgarian lunges, just like this one. The difference, of course, it that we're doing them in a specific sequence, and adding some things you probably haven't done before, but your coach or trainer should show you how to incorporate this program with your other work.

In my experience, coaches want you to be athletic, but they don't always train you to be athletic. They know how to teach specific skills and techniques for their sport; they can teach you certain moves and strategies; they can teach you how to play the game. But they expect their athletes to be athletic, and it's up to you to develop that athleticism. This program gives you everything you need to get there. If you do Jump Attack in your off-season, you will be a different athlete when you go back the following season. Just showing up for workouts doing some of these moves—the Lunge Buttkicker, the Attack Depth Jumps, the Seated Box Jump—will show your coaches how hard you've worked, how much you've improved, and how much you want to succeed.

I DON'T NEED THREE DAYS TO REST.
CAN I DO THE PROGRAM FASTER?

Doing more than prescribed will not give you faster results; it will actually slow your progress. No matter how you feel, you need the recovery days that are built into this program. Jump Attack requires maximum effort, and you can't give that with tired muscles. It's not a weakness to take days off, it's a necessity and the sign of a smart athlete.

I'M IN MY FOURTH WEEK AND I'M NOT SEEING RESULTS.
AM I DOING SOMETHING WRONG?

You probably won't see results by four weeks. In fact, if you test too soon, you may even see a decrease in your vertical jump while your new muscles are developing. Your muscles are starting to do something completely new; give them time to adapt.

As I said earlier—and I will say it again—it's not essential for you to test at all. I don't consider the vertical jump test to be a measure of success. But if you do plan to test yourself, I strongly suggest you test on Day 1 and then not again until after Day 90; don't test every week or every day or every phase. See chapter 9, "The Results," for more.

WHAT SHOULD I DO DURING THE REST AND RECOVERY WEEK?

At the end of every three-week phase, there's a week of rest. But rest doesn't mean lying on the couch eating cookies. It means play your sport, stay active, use your body. But no weight workouts. Give yourself a break from the intensity of this program; you will have earned it. You can read more about rest and recovery in chapter 8.

WILL JUMP ATTACK GIVE ME THE SKILLS TO EXCEL AT MY SPORT?

Here's the deal: We'll make you more explosive and athletic, and you'll use your new physical ability to master your skills so you can get to the next level.

This workout won't train you to shoot a ball or catch a pass; those are skill components you have to learn. Being explosive doesn't guarantee success; I've seen too many players come out of high school or college with great physical superiority, but no skills to match. It might help you get noticed because an explosive athlete is hard to miss, but if you can't play the game you'll eventually get noticed for that instead.

It works the other way too, by the way. You might have tremendous skill—ball handling, shooting, passing—but not explosiveness.

If you have the skills but lack athletic ability, there's no question that this program can be extremely beneficial to you.

Bottom line: Training your body isn't the same as training for your sport. MJ had all the physical tools to be the best, but what made him truly unstoppable was his work ethic and his mental toughness. He understood the importance of hard work and how to put the work to use in real games, in real life. Jump Attack gives you the blueprint to develop physical excellence; it's up to you how you use it to go beyond that.

IF I WANT TO TEST MY VERTICAL JUMP, WHEN SHOULD I DO THAT?

As you'll read many times in this book, an increased vertical jump is only one result of this workout, not the whole result. It is not essential for you to test yourself by jumping up to touch a wall; believe me, you'll see the results in your performance.

But if you *do* want to test your vertical jump, test on Day 1 before you begin this program, and test again on Day 90 (or five to seven days after you do the last leg workout). By waiting those five to seven days at the end, your legs should be fully rested, allowing you to get the maximum height on your vertical jump.

Resist testing yourself in the middle of the ninety-day program. You may actually see a decline in your measurement because your muscles will likely be tired; they'll still be developing and still learning what they're supposed to do.

For more details on how and when to test, see chapter 9, "The Results."

CHAPTER 6

THE JUMP ATTACK WORKOUT

PHASE 1

FIRE

Prepare the Muscles to Fire

PHASE 2

FORCE

Train to Create Force

PHASE 3

FLIGHT

Take Flight

JUMP ATTACK

PHASE 1: *FIRE*

Relentless Legs
Relentless Total Body

The first phase of the program got its name for two reasons: (1) we're preparing your muscles to fire, and (2) these exercises will make them feel like they're on fire.

During these three weeks, you'll begin elongating the muscles and teaching them to fire in the correct sequence. This is an especially crucial stage for young athletes who are still growing. We're getting your ligaments and tendons and joints ready for the next phase, when you'll start putting impact on your body. We're also preparing you to jump properly, with power and balance, so you're using all the muscles in your lower and upper body to maximize your explosiveness, not just jumping off one group of muscles—whether you're exploding straight up, to the side, backward, or for the second or third time. If you looked at pictures of the human body and highlighted 100 percent of the muscles needed to make you more explosive, we're training all of those right now.

The exercises in the Fire phase are all about stamina and mental toughness. We're using isometric moves to prepare your muscles, your ligaments, and your mind for what's ahead. During these exercises, you will likely feel the fire—a burning sensation in your muscles, like you've never felt before. It's temporary, and the more you think about it, the more it's going to burn. I'm challenging you mentally, because while the exercises look simple (such as getting into a lunge position and holding it), they take serious mental stamina. Can you hold it for sixty seconds? Can you hold it for ninety seconds? How about two minutes? You're going to find out, and test your ability to be comfortable being uncomfortable, because if you keep thinking about how much longer you have to hold that position, the clock is never going to move. It's like a staring contest: the more you think "Don't blink!" the more you want to blink. And because there's no motion in these exercises, all you can think about is how it feels to hold the move. Time goes slowly when you're waiting for it to speed up. Control time. Go somewhere else mentally. Find a song you can listen to and lose yourself, or envision the end result of your training or just tune in to the sound of your own breath. If you're thinking how hard it is, you will fail, and I'm not going to let you fail. Without a doubt, this is the part of the workout that makes people most likely want to quit before they really get going. When you get through this section—and you will—you will realize how mentally tough you really are, and what you are capable of achieving.

Tough from the neck up will make you tougher from the neck down.

PHASE 1: *FIRE*

TRAINING FOR MAXIMUM RESULTS

- *Important*: Read each description carefully, study the photos, and pay close attention to the details. How are the hands positioned? Where are the knees? How low are the hips? Where should you be looking? Feet together or apart? The form illustrated in the photos is accurate; your best results (and your lowest risk of injury) will come from duplicating that form.

- Small details make huge differences. Some of these look like exercises you've done before, but most have little changes that add up to big results. The slightest varia-tion—putting your foot on a plate, elevating a heel, turn-ing your wrists—will activate muscles you'd likely never focus on. So many people say, "But I was taught to do it this way." I already know that. I do it differently, and so do my clients. You can't be better than everyone else if you do things just like everyone else.

- Each sequence begins with a preexhaustion exercise and ends with a stretch; they are identical in each sequence. Do not skip them because you did them in the previ-ous sequence; they are there for a reason and essential for your success. We're preparing and stretching the hip area, because the looser your hips, the higher you'll jump. If you skip these moves, your hips will tighten and your jumping ability will be seriously limited.

- If you absolutely can't hold a position for the entire time, pause for a moment and allow the muscle to briefly recover. When you continue, start timing from when you paused; you must do the entire required time to complete the exercise and move on to the next one. Keep a record of how long you were able to hold the position before having to pause; you should last a few seconds longer each time, until you don't have to pause at all.

- Holding a position doesn't mean holding your breath. Remember to take slow, deep breaths, in through your nose, out through your mouth.

- During the sequences, we're alternating two different moves, three times each. Do a set of the first exercise, then a set of the other exercise, repeating for three sets of each. When only one exercise appears in a sequence, just do that one.

- You must be able to do all the hold moves for the full time specified before moving on to Phase 2. If you are unable to do so, repeat that week of the workout until you're ready to proceed.

- For exercises that begin on the left or the right:
  - For leg workouts: Day 1, start right leg. Day 4, start left leg.
  - For Total Body workouts: Day 2, start right. Day 5, start left.

- Most of these sequences include one Hold move and one Pump move; you will alternate them for three sets. You can rest for up to two minutes between sets, but the Hold/Pump combination should be done without a break. They are designed to be done together, with minimal rest in between.

- During each exercise, remember to squeeze the glutes and keep the abs tight.
- Record your results. You can make notes in the book, put all the data in your phone, get a notebook . . . just make sure you keep a journal of what you did each time so you know what to do next time. There is no better way to track your improvement.

PHASE 1: *FIRE*

Workout Schedule
Weeks 1–4

	DAY 1	DAY 2	DAY 3	DAY 4	DAY 5	DAY 6	DAY 7
WEEK 1	Relentless Legs Sequences 1–5	Relentless Total Body	Rest and Recovery	Relentless Legs Sequences 1–5	Relentless Total Body	Rest and Recovery	Rest and Recovery
WEEK 2	Relentless Legs Sequences 1–5	Relentless Total Body	Rest and Recovery	Relentless Legs Sequences 1–5	Relentless Total Body	Rest and Recovery	Rest and Recovery
WEEK 3	Relentless Legs Sequences 1–5	Relentless Total Body	Rest and Recovery	Relentless Legs Sequences 1–5	Relentless Total Body	Rest and Recovery	Rest and Recovery
WEEK 4	Recovery Week	Recovery Week	Recovery Week	Recovery Week	Recovery Week	Recovery Week	Recovery Week

PHASE 1: *FIRE*

RELENTLESS LEGS

Sequences 1–5

Day 1 and Day 4

SEQUENCE 1

Fire Hydrants

Do 10 times forward, 10 times backward, 10 times side.

Repeat on opposite leg.

Do 1 set.

Tiptoe Squat Hold

Week 1: 60 seconds.

Week 2: 90 seconds.

Week 3: 120 seconds.

Tiptoe Squat Pump

Week 1: 15 reps.

Week 2: 10 reps.

Week 3: 5 reps.

Alternate sets of Tiptoe Squat Holds and Tiptoe Squat Pumps. The Pumps are done immediately after the Holds, with minimal to no rest. You can rest up to 2 minutes between sets.

Repeat 3 times.

Hip Flexor Stretch

Do 30 seconds each side.

Do 1 set.

SEQUENCE 1 EXERCISES

FIRE HYDRANTS

This exercise repeats in sequences 1–5.

Day 1, start right leg. Day 4, start left leg.

10x forward
10x backward
10x side
Switch legs

Begin on your hands and knees. Back is neutral, abs and glutes are tight, arms directly under shoulders, knees directly under hips.

- With your knee bent, lift one leg laterally as high as possible without tilting the pelvis; keep the hips and shoulders square to the floor. Your knee must remain bent throughout the exercise, not straightened in back, so your heel stays close to your butt throughout the entire exercise. Lock into that position during the rotations.

- Rotate your hip in a circle forward 10 times, then backward 10 times, then to the side 10 times.
- Switch legs and repeat.

TIPTOE SQUAT HOLD

| Week 1: 60 seconds |
| Week 2: 90 seconds |
| Week 3: 120 seconds |

- Begin in a squat position, feet hip-width apart, thighs parallel to the floor, chest up, straight back, glutes squeezed tight.
- Elevate onto your toes, pressing them into the floor with as much force as possible. Your elbows are inside your knees, pushing out as your thighs push in. Hold the position.

TIPTOE SQUAT PUMP

Week 1: 15 reps
Week 2: 10 reps
Week 3: 5 reps

- Begin in the same position as the Tiptoe Squat Hold, but your elbows are above your knees.
- Raise and lower slightly, 3 to 5 inches, at a slow, controlled speed. Keep your knees bent and squeeze the glutes as hard as you can throughout the entire exercise. Do not stand straight up. Do not bounce.

HIP FLEXOR STRETCH

This exercise repeats in sequences 1–4.

Day 1, start right leg. Day 4, start left leg.

30 seconds each side

- Front foot on a 1-to-2-inch plate, front knee bent slightly deeper than 90 degrees, back knee on the floor, hips pressed forward.
- Using the hand opposite the back leg, pull the foot toward your butt, leaving the knee on the floor. Raise the other hand with a slight side bend overhead. Keep your hips pressed forward until you feel the stretch in the hip area. Hold for 30 seconds.
- Repeat on the opposite side.
- You may have difficulty pulling the back foot up to the butt at first; if so, continue doing this stretch anyway without raising the back foot. As your hips become looser throughout the program, you will see progress.

SEQUENCE 2

Fire Hydrants

Do 10 times forward, 10 times backward, 10 times side.

Repeat on opposite leg.

Do 1 set.

Lunge Hold

Week 1: 60 seconds.

Week 2: 90 seconds.

Week 3: 120 seconds.

Lunge Pump

Week 1: 15 reps.

Week 2: 10 reps.

Week 3: 5 reps.

Alternate sets of Lunge Holds and Lunge Pumps. The Pumps are done immediately after the Holds, with minimal to no rest. You can rest up to 2 minutes between sets.

Repeat 3 times.

Hip Flexor Stretch

Do 30 seconds each side.

Do 1 set.

SEQUENCE 2 EXERCISES

FIRE HYDRANTS

Pictured on page 72.

LUNGE HOLD

Week 1: 60 seconds
Week 2: 90 seconds
Week 3: 120 seconds

Stand with your front foot on a 1-to-2-inch plate, front knee bent slightly deeper than 90 degrees, thigh parallel to the floor, front heel elevated. Press the ball of your foot into the plate with as much force as possible. The back leg is as straight as possible, as low to the floor as possible, arms at your sides, glutes squeezed tight. Hold the position.

LUNGE PUMP

Week 1: 15 reps
Week 2: 10 reps
Week 3: 5 reps

Begin in the same position as the Lunge Hold. Then raise and lower slightly 3 to 5 inches at a slow, controlled speed, squeezing the glutes as hard as you can throughout the entire exercise. The back leg maintains the same lunge position. Do not stand.

HIP FLEXOR STRETCH

Pictured on page 75.

SEQUENCE 3

Fire Hydrants
Do 10 times forward, 10 times backward, 10 times side.

Repeat on opposite leg.

Do 1 set.

Elevated Bulgarian Lunge Hold
Week 1: 60 seconds.

Week 2: 90 seconds.

Week 3: 120 seconds.

Elevated Bulgarian Lunge Pump
Week 1: 15 reps.

Week 2: 10 reps.

Week 3: 5 reps.

Alternate sets of Elevated Bulgarian Lunge Holds and Elevated Bulgarian Lunge Pumps. The Pumps are done immediately after the Holds, with minimal to no rest. You can rest up to 2 minutes between sets.

Repeat 3 times.

Hip Flexor Stretch
Do 30 seconds each side.

Do 1 set.

SEQUENCE 3 EXERCISES

FIRE HYDRANTS

Pictured on page 72.

ELEVATED BULGARIAN LUNGE HOLD

Week 1: 60 seconds
Week 2: 90 seconds
Week 3: 120 seconds

- Begin with your front foot on a 1-to-2-inch plate, the front leg bent at approximately 90 degrees, the front heel elevated slightly so you're on your toes, pressing the ball of the foot into the plate with as much force as possible.
- Your back foot is elevated on a bench with the ball of your foot resting on the bench. The back leg is as straight as possible. Squeeze the glutes. Hold the position.

ELEVATED BULGARIAN LUNGE PUMP

Week 1: 15 reps
Week 2: 10 reps
Week 3: 5 reps

Begin in the same position as the Elevated Bulgarian Lunge Hold. Then raise and lower 3 to 5 inches at a slow, controlled speed, squeezing the glutes as hard as you can throughout the entire exercise. Do not stand all the way up; maintain the lunge position.

HIP FLEXOR STRETCH
Pictured on page 75.

SEQUENCE 4

Fire Hydrants
Do 10 times forward, 10 times backward, 10 times side.
Repeat on opposite leg.
Do 1 set.

Straight-Legged Dead Lift Hold
Week 1: 60 seconds.
Week 2: 90 seconds.
Week 3: 120 seconds.

Straight-Legged Dead Lift Pump
Week 1: 15 reps.
Week 2: 10 reps.
Week 3: 5 reps.

Alternate sets of Straight-Legged Dead Lift Holds and Straight-Legged Dead Lift Pumps. The Pumps are done immediately after the Holds, with minimal to no rest. You can rest up to 2 minutes between sets.
Repeat 3 times.

Hip Flexor Stretch
Do 30 seconds each side.
Do 1 set.

SEQUENCE 4 EXERCISES

FIRE HYDRANTS

See page 72.

STRAIGHT-LEGGED DEAD LIFT HOLD

| Week 1: 60 seconds |
| Week 2: 90 seconds |
| Week 3: 120 seconds |

Stand with your hips slightly back while holding dumbbells or a bar (total weight, 20 to 50 pounds) in front of your thighs.

Push the hips back slightly and bend at the hips with straight legs, chin tucked, back flat, shoulders back, lowering weights as close to the floor as possible without losing form. Glutes remain squeezed tight. Hold the position.

STRAIGHT-LEGGED DEAD LIFT PUMP

| Week 1: 15 reps |
| Week 2: 10 reps |
| Week 3: 5 reps |

Begin in the same bent position as the Straight-Legged Dead Lift Hold, then raise and lower the weights 8 to 10 inches at a slow, controlled speed without rounding your back or losing form. Do not stand all the way up.

HIP FLEXOR STRETCH

Pictured on page 75.

SEQUENCE 5

Fire Hydrants
Do 10 times forward, 10 times backward, 10 times side.
Repeat on opposite leg.
Do 1 set.

V-Up Hold
Week 1: 60 seconds.
Week 2: 90 seconds.
Week 3: 120 seconds.

V-Up Pump
Week 1: 15 reps.
Week 2: 10 reps.
Week 3: 5 reps.

Alternate sets of V-Up Holds and V-Up Pumps. The Pumps are done immediately after the Holds, with minimal to no rest. You can rest up to 2 minutes between sets.
Repeat 3 times.

V-Calf Stretch
Do 30 seconds each side.
Do 1 set.

SEQUENCE 5 EXERCISES

FIRE HYDRANTS

Pictured on page 72.

V-UP HOLD

Week 1: 60 seconds	
Week 2: 90 seconds	
Week 3: 120 seconds	

Place your palms and feet on the floor and your butt in the air, legs straight, glutes tight, hands as close to your feet as possible, so you are in an inverted V position. Raise on your toes as high as possible, tuck your chin, and hold the position.

V-UP PUMP

Week 1: 15 reps
Week 2: 10 reps
Week 3: 5 reps

Begin in the V-Up Hold position, then lower your heels as close to the floor as you can, and raise back up again. Keep the glutes tight.

V-CALF STRETCH

30 seconds each side

- Remain in an inverted V position following the V-Up Pump. Cross one leg behind the other, lower your heel to the floor, and hold. For a deeper stretch bring your hands closer to your feet.
- Switch legs and repeat.

PHASE 1: *FIRE*

RELENTLESS TOTAL BODY

Day 2 and Day 5

Note: The Total Body workouts are not done in sequences, so there is no preexhaustion exercise or stretch following each exercise.

Week 1: Do each exercise for 30 seconds.

Week 2: Do each exercise for 60 seconds.

Week 3: Do each exercise for 90 seconds.

Push-up Hold

Pull-up Hold

Alternate sets of each. Repeat 3 times.

Overhead Hold

Bicep Hold

Alternate sets of each. Repeat 3 times.

Tricep Push-up Hold

Frog Plank Hold

Alternate sets of each. Repeat 3 times.

Side Plank Hold

PUSH-UP HOLD

Week 1: 30 seconds
Week 2: 60 seconds
Week 3: 90 seconds

Begin in a hand plank position, on your toes with your abs and glutes tight, back straight, hands directly under your shoulders.

Lower as if you're doing a push-up. Bend your elbows to the sides as you lower your body, maintaining a straight line until your chest is 1 inch from the floor. Hold the position.

PULL-UP HOLD

Week 1:	30 seconds
Week 2:	60 seconds
Week 3:	90 seconds

With your palms facing away from you, hold the bar with your hands slightly wider than shoulder width, knees slightly bent (not tucked under you), and legs uncrossed.

- Pull yourself up so your chin is above the bar and shoulders are back. Hold the position.
- If you can't pull yourself up, you can jump up or use a step to get above the bar.

| Week 1: 30 seconds |
| Week 2: 60 seconds |
| Week 3: 90 seconds |

- You can use a barbell or dumbbells for this exercise.
- Stand with your feet shoulder-width apart, hips slightly back, weights at your shoulders, palms facing away from you.

Lift the weights straight overhead, locking the elbows and squeezing the glutes. Hold the position.

BICEP HOLD

| Week 1: 30 seconds |
| Week 2: 60 seconds |
| Week 3: 90 seconds |

Hold the dumbbells at your sides, wrists straight, palms facing away from you. Abs and glutes are tight.

Raise the dumbbells slightly more than halfway to your shoulders but not all the way up; the elbows do not move forward or back. Hold the position.

TRICEP PUSH-UP HOLD

Week 1: 30 seconds
Week 2: 60 seconds
Week 3: 90 seconds

Begin in an elbow plank position on your toes, hands slightly extended in front of your shoulders, fingers pointing forward.

Raise your elbows and forearms until the elbows are about 2 inches off the floor. Keep your back straight and your abs and glutes tight. Hold the position.

FROG PLANK HOLD

Day 2, begin right side. Day 5, begin left side.

Week 1: 30 seconds
Week 2: 60 seconds
Week 3: 90 seconds

Begin in an elbow plank position on your toes, abs and glutes tight, back straight. Open palms face each other, shoulder-width apart; do not make a fist. Elevate one foot.

- Bring one knee up and around as close to your elbow as possible, toes pointed to the side, maintaining your arms at a 90-degree angle. Hold the position for the required time.
- Switch legs and repeat on the other side.

SIDE PLANK HOLD

Week 1:	30 seconds
Week 2:	60 seconds
Week 3:	90 seconds

Begin in a side plank position on one elbow, opposite arm overhead, abs and glutes tight, back straight, feet stacked one on top of the other. Don't allow your hips to sink toward the floor.

- Bend your top knee toward your chest. Your foot is flexed, not pointed. Hold the position for the required time.
- Switch sides and repeat.

PHASE 1: *FIRE*

Rest and Recovery
Days 3, 6, and 7, and all of Week 4

The Rest and Recovery Days and the full Recovery Week at the end of each phase are essential for helping your body get ready for the challenges ahead; they are as important to your success as the days you're actually working out. You don't build new muscle during your workouts; you actually tear it down while you train. The new muscle is built while you sleep and rest. Don't deprive yourself of that opportunity.

On these days, continue to use your body: play your sport, stay active, but no weight training. Give the muscles a rest from the intense work you've been doing. You can't get your best results if you're too fatigued to give your best effort.

Just remember, if you haven't done enough to create the need for rest and recovery, these days will just become "off days" from which you'll get zero benefit. If you want to make real progress, be sure you're working hard enough so your body has a reason to recover.

See chapter 8, on rest, recovery, and injuries, for further discussion.

PHASE 2: *FORCE*

Power Legs
Power Total Body

Your body is now ready for Phase 2: We begin attacking the muscles harder, combining weights and plyo for unmatched explosiveness. Be ready to overload the muscles, getting them ready to apply more force into the floor and testing your ability to push yourself harder than you ever have.

In Phase 1 we worked on lengthening the muscles; now we're working on shortening them as well. Most programs will give you one or the other, but you need both to be explosive. Remember, the faster you can get the muscle to lengthen and shorten, the more explosive you'll be; just like snapping the rubber band, the quicker you can stretch it and release it, the harder it snaps.

Here you're going to experience the unmistakable power of the Explosive Sequences. Instead of doing all your weights and then all your plyometrics on different days, we're going to superset them: a weight exercise immediately followed by a plyo exercise. You're acclimating the muscles to explosiveness, training them to reflexively attack the movement.

For the weight exercises, you're holding a position (just as you did in Phase 1) and immediately exploding into a set of reps, teaching your body to create explosive action.

The plyo exercises aren't just about jumping in the air; we're also training your body to land, absorb the impact, and explode back into the air. You will learn to move more quickly and jump higher, not just on your first jump but on your second and third as well.

The first time you do some of these moves, you will probably find them extremely challenging. You will see progress each week if you stick with it, finish all the reps, and give your maximum effort each time. We're not here to make it easy. We're here to get results.

PHASE 2: *FORCE*

TRAINING FOR MAXIMUM RESULTS

- *Important*: Read each description carefully, study the photos, and pay close attention to the details. How are the hands positioned? Where are the knees? How low are the hips? Where should you be looking? Feet together or apart? The form illustrated in the photos is accurate; your best results (and your lowest risk of injury) will come from duplicating that form.

- Small details make huge differences. Some of these look like exercises you've done before, but most have little changes that add up to big results. The slightest variation—putting your foot on a plate, elevating a heel, turning your wrists—will activate muscles you'd likely never focus on. So many people say, "But I was taught to do it this way." I already know that, I do it differently, and so do my clients. You can't be better than everyone else if you do things just like everyone else.

- Each sequence begins with a preexhaustion exercise and ends with a stretch; they are identical in each sequence. Do not skip them because you did them in the previous sequence; they are there for a reason and essential for your success. We're preparing and stretching the hip area, because the looser your hips, the higher you'll jump. If you skip these moves, your hips will tighten and your jumping ability will be seriously limited.

- For the Force phase, choose weights that are challenging for you, slightly lighter than you normally use for weight training. You can always go up, and you will; increase the amount of weight you lift each week, and between sets if you can, but make sure you maintain your form. If you're struggling, the weight is too heavy. If you're not feeling the effort, the weight is too light. The amount of weight you lift is much less important than moving it correctly.

- Remember, we're going for explosive speed; this is not a weight-lifting program. I don't care how much you can lift, I care about how quickly you can move the weight from here to there. That's how you become explosive: speed, not bulk.

- If an exercise is too challenging for you at first, keep working. You will get there. Jump Attack is a progression; by the end of each phase, you're already doing things you couldn't do at the beginning. If you can't do an exercise for the entire time, pause for a moment, then continue. Your body may want to quit but your mind calls the shots. Finish what you start.

- The exercises are done in supersets, meaning we're alternating two different moves, three times each. Do a set of the first exercise, then a set of the other exercise, repeating for three sets of each. When only one exercise appears in a sequence, do that one.

- Remember to squeeze the glutes and keep the abs tight throughout every exercise.

- For exercises that begin on the left or the right:
  - For leg workouts: Day 1, start right leg. Day 4, start left leg.

- For Total Body workouts: Day 2, start right. Day 5, start left.

Rest briefly—one minute or less—between each exercise and two minutes between each set.

Record your results. You can make notes in the book, put all the data in your phone, get a notebook . . . just make sure you keep a journal of what you did each time so you know what to do next time. There is no better way to track your improvement.

PHASE 2: *FORCE*

Workout Schedule
Weeks 5–8

	DAY 1	DAY 2	DAY 3	DAY 4	DAY 5	DAY 6	DAY 7
WEEK 5	Power Legs Sequences 6–10	Power Total Body	Rest and Recovery	Power Legs Sequences 6–10	Power Total Body	Rest and Recovery	Rest and Recovery
WEEK 6	Power Legs Sequences 6–10	Power Total Body	Rest and Recovery	Power Legs Sequences 6–10	Power Total Body	Rest and Recovery	Rest and Recovery
WEEK 7	Power Legs Sequences 6–10	Power Total Body	Rest and Recovery	Power Legs Sequences 6–10	Power Total Body	Rest and Recovery	Rest and Recovery
WEEK 8	Recovery Week	Recovery Week	Recovery Week	Recovery Week	Recovery Week	Recovery Week	Recovery Week

PHASE 2: *FORCE*

POWER LEGS

Sequences 6–10
Day 1 and Day 4

SEQUENCE 6

Glute Bridge
Do 15 each side.
Do 1 set.

Sitting Squats
Week 5: Hold for 30 seconds; then immediately do 10 reps.
Week 6: Hold for 20 seconds; then immediately do 10 reps.
Week 7: Hold for 10 seconds; then immediately do 10 reps.

Lunge Buttkickers
Week 5: Do 10 reps on one side; repeat on the other side.
Week 6: Do 8 reps on one side; repeat on the other side.
Week 7: Do 6 reps on one side; repeat on the other side.

Alternate sets of Sitting Squats and Lunge Buttkickers.
Repeat 3 times.

Hip Flexor Stretch
Do 30 seconds each side.
Do 1 set.

SEQUENCE 6 EXERCISES

GLUTE BRIDGE

Day 1, begin right side. Day 4, begin left side.

15 reps each side

Lie on your back with your knees bent, feet flat on the floor shoulder-width apart, glutes tight, fingers pointed to the ceiling.

- Elevate your hips as high as possible. Pull one knee toward your chest, with your opposite foot on the floor, resting on your heel. Your toes are pointed up.
- Raise and lower your hips in a slow and controlled motion. Go as low as you can to the floor without touching the floor.
- Do 15 reps on one side, then return to the start position and begin again on the other side.

SITTING SQUATS

Week 5: Hold 30 seconds, then 10 reps
Week 6: Hold 20 seconds, then 10 reps
Week 7: Hold 10 seconds, then 10 reps

- For this exercise, a barbell is preferable, but dumbbells are okay if a bar is not available.
- Begin with your feet shoulder-width apart, hips slightly back, heels elevated 1 to 2 inches onto a plate. Place the weight behind your neck so it rests on your shoulders.

- Push your hips back and slowly lower until you're 1 inch from the bench, but not actually sitting. Look straight ahead. Don't lean forward. Hold this position for the specified time.
- Then immediately begin the reps: Sit momentarily, pause, then explode to a standing position. Repeat for 10 reps.
- Increase the weight for each set, or as you are able.

LUNGE BUTTKICKERS

Week 5: 10 reps each side
Week 6: 8 reps each side
Week 7: 6 reps each side

Begin in a lunge position, with your front leg at a 90-degree angle, and your back leg extended with the knee slightly bent.

With a quick dip down for momentum, jump straight up for maximum height, kicking both heels to the butt.

- Land in the same beginning lunge position, keeping your balance so you can stick the landing.
- If necessary, reposition your front leg to a 90-degree angle before repeating.
- Do not alternate; use the same leg for all reps. Then switch legs.

HIP FLEXOR STRETCH

This exercise repeats in sequences 6–9.

Day 1, start right leg. Day 4, start left leg.

30 seconds each side

- Begin with your front foot on a 1-to-2-inch plate, front knee bent slightly deeper than 90 degrees, back knee on the floor, hips pressed forward.
- Using the hand opposite of the back leg, pull the foot toward the butt, leaving the knee on the floor. Raise the other hand with a slight side bend overhead. Keep your hips pressed forward until you feel the stretch in the hip area. Hold for 30 seconds.
- Repeat on the opposite side.
- You may have difficulty pulling the back foot up to the butt at first; if so, continue doing this stretch anyway without raising the back foot. As your hips become looser throughout the program, you will see progress.

SEQUENCE 7

Glute Bridge
Do 15 each side.
Do 1 set.

Reverse Lunge
Week 5: Hold for 30 seconds; then immediately do 10 reps.
   Repeat on the other leg.
Week 6: Hold for 20 seconds; then immediately do 10 reps.
   Repeat on the other leg.
Week 7: Hold for 10 seconds; then immediately do 10 reps.
   Repeat on the other leg.

Tuck Jumps
Week 5: Do 10 reps.
Week 6: Do 8 reps.
Week 7: Do 6 reps.

Alternate sets of Reverse Lunges and Tuck Jumps.
Repeat 3 times.

Hip Flexor Stretch
Do 30 seconds each side.
Do 1 set.

GLUTE BRIDGE

Pictured on page 106.

REVERSE LUNGE

Week 5: Hold 30 seconds, then 10 reps
Week 6: Hold 20 seconds, then 10 reps
Week 7: Hold 10 seconds, then 10 reps

Holding dumbbells at your sides, stand with both feet on a 1-to-2-inch plate or platform.

- Step back with one foot into a lunge so your front thigh is parallel to the floor, knee bent slightly deeper than 90 degrees, back leg as straight as possible so your knee does not touch the floor. Hold the position for the specified time.
- Then immediately return to the starting position, and do 10 reps on the same leg, in a slow, controlled motion. Switch legs and repeat the hold and reps on the other leg.
- Increase the weight for each set, or as you are able.

TUCK JUMPS

| Week 5: 10 reps |
| Week 6: 8 reps |
| Week 7: 6 reps |

Stand with your knees slightly bent, arms at your sides.

Dip down as quickly as possible to give you momentum right before you jump; this is a fast down-up move without hesitation before you jump.

Jump straight up as high as you can, hugging your knees to your chest, and release back down. Be sure you bring your knees to your chest, not your chest down to your knees.

- Land with your hips above your knees without dropping your butt to the floor.
- Make sure you return to the beginning standing position before repeating.

HIP FLEXOR STRETCH

Pictured on page 112.

SEQUENCE 8

Glute Bridge
Do 15 each side.
Do 1 set.

Burpee Dead Lifts
Week 5: Hold the plank position for 30 seconds, then
   immediately do 10 Burpee Dead Lifts.
Week 6: Hold the plank position for 20 seconds, then
   immediately do 10 Burpee Dead Lifts.
Week 7: Hold the plank position for 10 seconds, then
   immediately do 10 Burpee Dead Lifts.

Seated Box Jumps
Week 5: Do 10 reps (18-to-24-inch box).
Week 6: Do 8 reps (24-to-36-inch box).
Week 7: Do 6 reps (36-to-42-inch box).

Alternate sets of Burpee Dead Lifts and Seated Box Jumps.
Repeat 3 times.

Hip Flexor Stretch
Do 30 seconds each side.
Do 1 set.

SEQUENCE 8 EXERCISES

GLUTE BRIDGE

Pictured on page 106.

BURPEE DEAD LIFTS

Week 5: Hold plank 30 seconds, then 10 Burpee Dead Lifts
Week 6: Hold plank 20 seconds, then 10 Burpee Dead Lifts
Week 7: Hold plank 10 seconds, then 10 Burpee Dead Lifts

Hold the straight-arm plank position on the bar, hands slightly wider than your shoulders, feet hip-width apart. Glutes are tight throughout entire exercise. If necessary, place a towel or wedge in front of the weights to prevent the barbell from rolling. Hold for the specified time.

Then, still holding the bar, jump your feet in toward to the bar, knees bent.

Holding the bar as close to your legs as possible, with arms straight, stand up using your legs and hips, not your lower back. The bar is now at your thighs.

Reverse the motion, returning the bar to the floor.

- Feet jump back to the starting plank position. Repeat the above steps for 10 reps.
- Increase the weight for each set, or as you are able.

SEATED BOX JUMPS

| Week 5: 10 reps (18–24" box) |
| Week 6: 8 reps (24–36" box) |
| Week 7: 6 reps (36–42" box) |

Sit on a bench with your feet shoulder-width apart, toes pointed up, knees at a 90-degree angle. Without rocking back, bring your arms back for momentum.

- Transfer your weight to the balls of your feet, and jump up onto the box/platform. Land on the balls of your feet. Then stand up straight.
- Step down, return to the start position, and repeat.

HIP FLEXOR STRETCH

Pictured on page 112.

SEQUENCE 9

Glute Bridge
Do 15 each side.

Do 1 set.

Straight-Legged Dead Lifts
Week 5: Hold for 30 seconds; then immediately do 10 reps.

Week 6: Hold for 20 seconds; then immediately do 10 reps.

Week 7: Hold for 10 seconds; then immediately do 10 reps.

One-Legged Buttkickers
Week 5: Do 10 reps on one leg; repeat on the other side.

Week 6: Do 8 reps on one leg; repeat on the other side.

Week 7: Do 6 reps on one leg; repeat on the other side.

Alternate sets of Straight-Legged Dead Lifts and One-Legged Buttkickers.

Repeat 3 times.

Hip Flexor Stretch
Do 30 seconds each side.

Do 1 set.

SEQUENCE 9 EXERCISES

GLUTE BRIDGE

Pictured on page 106.

STRAIGHT-LEGGED DEAD LIFTS

| Week 5: Hold 30 seconds, then 10 reps |
| Week 6: Hold 20 seconds, then 10 reps |
| Week 7: Hold 10 seconds, then 10 reps |

Stand with your hips slightly back, holding a barbell in front of your thighs.

Push hips back slightly and bend at the hips with straight legs, back flat, shoulders back, chin tucked, glutes tight. Keep the bar close to your body, and lower the bar until it is directly over your feet, without touching the floor. Hold for the specified time.

- Then return to standing and do 10 reps.
- Increase the weight for each set, or as you are able.

ONE-LEGGED BUTTKICKERS

| Week 5: 10 reps each side |
| Week 6: 8 reps each side |
| Week 7: 6 reps each side |

Begin standing on one foot, with the opposite leg slightly bent behind you. The foot on the floor is going to do the work here.

- With a quick dip for momentum, jump up and kick your butt with the foot that was on the floor. Land on the same foot.
- Work for maximum height on each jump.
- Repeat as quickly as possible for a complete set on one side; repeat on the other side.

HIP FLEXOR STRETCH

Pictured on page 112.

SEQUENCE 10

Glute Bridge
Do 15 each side.

Do 1 set.

Weighted Calf Raises
Week 5: Hold for 30 seconds; then immediately do 15 reps.

Week 6: Hold for 20 seconds; then immediately do 15 reps.

Week 7: Hold for 10 seconds; then immediately do 15 reps.

Do 3 sets.

Calf Stretch
Do 30 seconds each side.

Do 1 set.

SEQUENCE 10 EXERCISES

GLUTE BRIDGE

Pictured on page 106.

WEIGHTED CALF RAISES

Week 5: Hold 30 seconds, then 15 reps
Week 6: Hold 20 seconds, then 15 reps
Week 7: Hold 10 seconds, then 15 reps

Stand with your toes on a plate, heels on the floor, barbell resting behind your neck on your shoulders.

- Explode up onto your toes to maximum height and hold for the specified time.
- Then lower your heels in a controlled manner and repeat for 15 reps.
- Increase the weight for each set, or as you are able.

CALF STRETCH

30 seconds each side

- Without weights, stand with one foot on a plate (at least 4 inches off the floor), heel over the edge.
- Slowly lower your heel off the plate until you feel a stretch in your calf. Hold without pulsing or bouncing.
- Switch legs and repeat.

PHASE 2: *FORCE*

POWER TOTAL BODY

Day 2 and Day 5

Note: The Total Body workouts are not done in sequences, so there is no preexhaustion exercise or stretch following each exercise.

For exercises using weights, choose weights that are challenging but allow you to keep your form. Increase the weight for each set, or as you are able.

Week 5: Hold each position 30 seconds; then immediately do 10 reps.

Week 6: Hold each position 60 seconds; then immediately do 10 reps.

Week 7: Hold each position 90 seconds; then immediately do 10 reps.

Push-up Hold with 10 Reps

Pull-up Hold with 10 Reps

Alternate sets of each. Repeat 3 times.

Overhead Hold with 10 Reps

Bicep Hold with 10 Reps

Alternate sets of each. Repeat 3 times.

Tricep Push-up Hold with 10 Reps

Frog Plank Hold with 10 Reps

Alternate sets of each. Repeat 3 times.

Side Plank Hold with 10 Reps

POWER TOTAL BODY EXERCISES

PUSH-UP HOLD WITH 10 REPS

Week 5: Hold 30 seconds, then 10 reps
Week 6: Hold 60 seconds, then 10 reps
Week 7: Hold 90 seconds, then 10 reps

Begin in the hand plank position, on your toes with your abs and glutes tight, back straight, hands directly under your shoulders.

Lower as if you're doing a push-up. Bend your elbows to the sides as you lower your body, maintaining a straight line until your chest is 1 inch from the floor. Hold the position for the specified time; then immediately do 10 push-ups.

PULL-UP HOLD WITH 10 REPS

Week 5: Hold 30 seconds, then 10 reps	
Week 6: Hold 60 seconds, then 10 reps	
Week 7: Hold 90 seconds, then 10 reps	

With your palms facing away from you, hold the bar with your hands slightly wider than shoulder width, knees slightly bent (not tucked under you), and legs uncrossed.

Pull yourself up so your chin is above the bar, shoulders back. Hold the position for the specified time; then immediately do 10 pull-ups.

OVERHEAD HOLD WITH 10 REPS

| Week 5: Hold 30 seconds, then 10 reps |
| Week 6: Hold 60 seconds, then 10 reps |
| Week 7: Hold 90 seconds, then 10 reps |

- You can use a barbell or dumbbells for this exercise.
- Stand with your feet shoulder-width apart, hips slightly back, weights at your shoulders, palms facing away from you.

- Lift the weights straight overhead and hold the position for the specified time. Then immediately lower the weights to your shoulders, knees slightly bent, and explode back up to the overhead position for 10 reps.
- Increase the weight for each set, or as you are able.

BICEP HOLD WITH 10 REPS

Week 5: Hold 30 seconds, then 10 reps
Week 6: Hold 60 seconds, then 10 reps
Week 7: Hold 90 seconds, then 10 reps

Hold dumbbells at your sides, wrists straight, palms facing away from you.

- Raise the dumbbells slightly more than halfway to your shoulders, but not all the way up; your elbows do not move forward or back, palms should be facing you. Hold

the position for the specified length of time; then lower
and raise the weights for 10 reps.

- Increase the weight for each set, or as you are able.

TRICEP PUSH-UP HOLD WITH 10 REPS

| Week 5: Hold 30 seconds, then 10 reps |
| Week 6: Hold 60 seconds, then 10 reps |
| Week 7: Hold 90 seconds, then 10 reps |

Begin in an elbow plank position on your toes, hands slightly
extended in front of your shoulders, fingers pointing forward, glutes
squeezed tight.

- Raise your elbows and forearms until the elbows are about
  2 inches off the floor. Keep your back straight and your
  abs tight. Hold the position for the specified time.

- Then immediately raise to a hand plank and begin fore-arm push-ups, lowering your forearms all the way to the floor (so you're in an elbow plank) and pushing back up again to a hand plank for 10 reps.
- Don't allow your hands to roll outward; keep your index fingers and thumbs firmly planted on the floor.

FROG PLANK HOLD WITH 10 REPS

Day 2, begin right side. Day 5, begin left side.

Week 5: Hold 30 seconds, then 10 reps
Week 6: Hold 60 seconds, then 10 reps
Week 7: Hold 90 seconds, then 10 reps

Begin in an elbow plank position on your toes, abs and glutes tight, back straight. Open palms face each other, shoulder-width apart; do not make a fist. Elevate one foot.

Bring one knee up and around as close to your elbow as possible, toes pointed to the side, maintaining your arms at a 90-degree angle. Hold the position for the specified time.

- Then immediately extend the bent leg straight back without touching the floor, and return it to the knee again for 10 reps.
- Switch legs and repeat the hold and reps on the other side.

SIDE PLANK HOLD WITH 10 REPS

Week 5: Hold 30 seconds, then 10 reps	
Week 6: Hold 60 seconds, then 10 reps	
Week 7: Hold 90 seconds, then 10 reps	

Begin in a side plank position on one elbow, opposite arm overhead, abs and glutes tight, back straight, feet stacked one on top of the other. Don't allow your hips to sink toward the floor.

Bend your top knee toward your chest. Your foot is flexed, not pointed. Hold the position for the specified time.

- Then rotate your torso (keeping the leg elevated and knee bent) until your shoulders are square to the floor and your arm is fully extended under your chest.
- Return to the previous position and repeat for 10 reps.
- Switch sides and repeat.

PHASE 2: *FORCE*

Rest and Recovery
Days 3, 6, and 7, and all of Week 8

The Rest and Recovery Days and the full Recovery Week at the end of each phase are essential for helping your body get ready for the challenges ahead; they are as important to your success as the days you're actually working out. You can't get your best results if you're too fatigued to give your best effort. On these days, continue to use your body: play your sport, stay active, but no weight training. Give the muscles a rest from the intense work you've been doing.

And give your body a chance to build new muscle. That doesn't happen during your workouts; you're actually breaking down muscle while you train. The new muscle is built while you sleep, while you rest. Don't deprive yourself of that opportunity.

But remember, if you haven't done enough to create the need for rest and recovery, these days will just become "off days" from which you'll get zero benefit. If you want to make real progress, be sure you're working hard enough so your body has a reason to recover.

See chapter 8, on rest, recovery, and injuries, for further discussion.

PHASE 3: *FLIGHT*

Explosive Legs
Explosive Total Body

Finally, what you've all been waiting for . . . Attack Depth Jumps!

By now you understand that we've been laying the foundation for the hardest work, training your body in a very specific way. You are now ready for flight; your muscles have been trained to create enough force to take off, and absorb force when you land so you can take off again—*that* is the definition of maximum explosiveness. Not just one jump straight up, but relentless power in all directions, over and over.

Phase 3 combines your new explosiveness with speed: We're timing how many reps you can do in a set time. You're not just jumping; you're executing the jump for quickness and rapid-fire repetition.

This phase prepares you for the ultimate challenge—game-time performance. It's one thing to jump around in a workout; it's another thing to jump in a real-time situation. We need your muscles to be so ready and prepared that when it's time to explode into action, you don't have to think about it. We're training your reflexes to take over, so when you have to move, your muscles know how to attack that movement quickly and powerfully.

Everything you've done in the first two phases makes it possible for you to do the exercises in this phase. If you had tried the Attack Depth Jumps at the beginning of the program, for example, you would have quit after a day; your body wasn't yet prepared to land properly, your hips, knees, and ankles wouldn't have been prepared for the challenge. Now they are. We haven't just been training you to jump, we've been working to develop your ability to land and explode back up . . . absorbing force and creating new force.

And all the core work you've done in Phases 1 and 2 pays off here too; these exercises require total body strength. Many people think of the core as just the abdominal region or "six-pack." In fact, the core includes everything from the chest to just above the knees, front and back. A strong core supports your whole body, and you need that now: As your muscles become more developed and you're able to jump higher, you're also putting more stress on your hips and knees and joints; your ligaments and joints now have to absorb a lot of impact and force as you repeatedly strike the floor and rebound. A strong core helps prevent injury as you challenge your body in new ways. You did all the work in the first two phases to lay the foundation.

It's time to fly.

PHASE 3: *FLIGHT*

TRAINING FOR MAXIMUM RESULTS

- *Important*: Read each description carefully, study the photos, and pay close attention to the details. How are the hands positioned? Where are the knees? How low are the hips? Where should you be looking? Feet together or apart? The form illustrated in the photos is accurate; your best results (and your lowest risk of injury) will come from duplicating that form.

- Small details make huge differences. Some of these look like exercises you've done before, but most have little changes that add up to big results. The slightest variation—putting your foot on a plate, elevating a heel, turning your wrists—will activate muscles you'd likely never focus on.

- Each sequence begins with a preexhaustion exercise and ends with a stretch; they are identical in each sequence. Do not skip them just because you did them in the previous sequence; they are there for a reason and essential for your success. We're preparing and stretching the hip area, because the looser your hips, the higher you'll jump. If you skip these moves, your hips will tighten and your jumping ability will be seriously limited.

- In this phase, choose weights that are heavier than the weights you used in the previous phase, but not so heavy that you sacrifice your form. Now we're lifting with speed to see how many reps you can do in 30 seconds; the amount of weight you lift is less important than your ability to move it correctly, but heavier weight with correct form will give you better results. You can always go up, and you will; increase the amount of weight you lift each week, and between sets if you can, but make sure you are able to maintain your form. If you're struggling, the weight is too heavy. If you're not feeling it, the weight is too light.

- Remember, we're going for explosive speed; this is not a weight-lifting program. I don't care how much you can lift. I care about how quickly you can move the weight from here to there. That's how you become explosive: speed, not bulk.

- If an exercise is too challenging for you at first, keep working. You will get there. Jump Attack is a progression; by the end of this third phase you're doing things you couldn't do at the beginning. If you can't do an exercise for the entire time, pause for a moment and continue. Finish what you start.

- The exercises are done in supersets, meaning we're going to alternate two different moves, three times each. Do a set of the first exercise, then a set of the other exercise, repeating for three sets of each. When only one exercise appears in a sequence, just do that one.

- For exercises that begin on the left or the right:
  - For leg workouts: Day 1, start right leg. Day 4, start left leg.
  - For Total Body workouts: Day 2, start right. Day 5, start left.

- Rest one minute between each exercise, and two minutes between each set.

- Remember to squeeze the glutes and keep the abs tight throughout every exercise.
- Even though you will have completed the exercises after Week 11, give yourself until Week 12 to see the full results of your work and to fully recover before resuming an intense training program.
- Record your results. There is no better way to track your improvement.
- And as always, all jumps are for maximum height, not speed.

PHASE 3: *FLIGHT*

Workout Schedule
Weeks 9–12

	DAY 1	DAY 2	DAY 3	DAY 4	DAY 5	DAY 6	DAY 7
WEEK 9	Explosive Legs Sequences 11-15	Explosive Total Body	Rest and Recovery	Explosive Legs Sequences 11-15	Explosive Total Body	Rest and Recovery	Rest and Recovery
WEEK 10	Explosive Legs Sequences 11-15	Explosive Total Body	Rest and Recovery	Explosive Legs Sequences 11-15	Explosive Total Body	Rest and Recovery	Rest and Recovery
WEEK 11	Explosive Legs Sequences 11-15	Explosive Total Body	Rest and Recovery	Explosive Legs Sequences 11-15	Explosive Total Body	Rest and Recovery	Rest and Recovery
WEEK 12	Recovery Week	Recovery Week	Recovery Week	Recovery Week	Recovery Week	Recovery Week	Recovery Week

PHASE 3: *FORCE*

EXPLOSIVE LEGS

Sequences 11–15
Day 1 and Day 4

SEQUENCE 11

Fire Hydrant/Bridge Walkout Combo

Do 10 times forward, 10 times backward, 10 times side.

Repeat on the opposite leg.

Then do 6-step Bridge Walkouts. Repeat 3 times.

Do 1 set.

Dead Lift

Week 9: Max reps for 30 seconds.

Week 10: Max reps for 20 seconds.

Week 11: Max reps for 15 seconds.

Alternating Buttkicker Scissors

Week 9: Do 10 reps, alternating legs (1 jump equals 1 rep).

Week 10: Do 8 reps, alternating legs (1 jump equals 1 rep).

Week 11: Do 6 reps, alternating legs (1 jump equals 1 rep).

Alternate sets of Dead Lifts and Alternating Buttkicker Scissors.
Repeat 3 times.

Hip Flexor Stretch

Do 30 seconds each side.

Do 1 set.

SEQUENCE 11 EXERCISES

FIRE HYDRANT/BRIDGE WALKOUT COMBO

Day 1, start right leg. Day 4, start left leg.

10x forward, 10x backward, 10x side, each leg
Then 3 Bridge Walkouts

Begin on your hands and knees. Your back is neutral, abs and glutes are tight, arms directly under your shoulders, knees directly under your hips.

- With your knee bent, lift one leg laterally as high as possible without tilting your pelvis; keep your hips and shoulders square to the floor. Your knee must remain bent throughout the exercise, not straightened in back, so your heel stays close to your butt throughout the entire exercise. Lock into that position during the rotations.

- Rotate your hip in a circle forward 10 times, then backward 10 times, then to the side 10 times.
- Repeat on the opposite leg.

Then immediately move onto your back for the Bridge Walkout:

- Your feet are on the floor hip-width apart, knees bent, and hips elevated as high as possible. You are on your heels with your toes pointed up. Your glutes stay contracted through the entire exercise. Your arms remain at your sides.
- Use your heels to walk your feet away from you for 6 alternating steps (3 on each side) until your legs are as straight as possible but your butt does not touch the floor at any time.
- Pause and walk back to the start position, using the same 6 alternating steps. Repeat 3 times.

DEAD LIFT

Week 9: 30 seconds
Week 10: 20 seconds
Week 11: 15 seconds

Begin with a barbell at your feet, hands on the bar outside your knees, chest up high, back flat, glutes tight, bar close to your shins.

- Lift to a standing position, thrusting your hips slightly forward, using your legs, hips, butt, and thighs to stand, not your lower back muscles.
- To reverse, push your hips slightly back, and return to the start position, lowering the bar to the floor, pushing your hips straight back and bending at the knees. Keep the bar as close to your legs as possible.
- Increase the weight for each set, or as you are able, while maintaining or increasing the number of reps.

ALTERNATING BUTTKICKER SCISSORS

Week 9: 10 reps	
Week 10: 8 reps	
Week 11: 6 reps	

Begin standing with your feet shoulder-width apart. You will return to this position for each rep.

Dip quickly before jumping, to give yourself momentum. This is a quick move, without hesitating before the jump.

Jump straight up for maximum height and kick both heels to your butt.

As you land, split your legs into a lunge position and land in a lunge. Do not lean forward. Your front leg should be bent at a 90-degree angle on landing.

Then return to the start position, repeat, and land on the opposite leg. Alternate legs for each rep.

HIP FLEXOR STRETCH

This exercise repeats in Sequences 11–14.

Day 1, start right leg. Day 4, start left leg.

30 seconds each side

- Begin with your front foot on a 1-to-2-inch plate, front knee bent slightly deeper than 90 degrees, back knee on the floor, hips pressed forward.
- Using the hand opposite the back leg, pull the foot toward the butt, leaving the knee on the floor. Raise the other hand with a slight side bend overhead. Keep your hips pressed forward until you feel the stretch in the hip area. Hold for 30 seconds.
- Repeat on the opposite side.

If you still have difficulty pulling the back foot up to the butt at first, continue doing this stretch anyway without raising the back foot. You will still get results, although you'll get better results with the extra stretch. Keep working!

SEQUENCE 12

Fire Hydrant/Bridge Walkout Combo

Do 10 times forward, 10 times backward, 10 times side.

Repeat on the opposite leg.

Then do 6-step Bridge Walkouts. Repeat 3 times.

Do 1 set.

Squats

Week 9: Max reps for 30 seconds.

Week 10: Max reps for 20 seconds.

Week 11: Max reps for 15 seconds.

Back Roll Tuck Jumps

Week 9: Do 10 reps.

Week 10: Do 8 reps.

Week 11: Do 6 reps.

Alternate sets of Squats and Back Roll Tuck Jumps.
Repeat 3 times.

Hip Flexor Stretch

Do 30 seconds each side.

Do 1 set.

SEQUENCE 12 EXERCISES

FIRE HYDRANT/BRIDGE WALKOUT COMBO
Pictured on pages 154–55.

SQUATS

| Week 9: 30 seconds |
| Week 10: 20 seconds |
| Week 11: 15 seconds |

Begin with your feet shoulder-width apart, hips slightly back, heels elevated 1 to 2 inches onto a plate. Place the weight behind your neck, resting it on your shoulders.

- With complete control, push your hips back and lower until your knees are bent at 90 degrees or slightly more and your thighs are parallel to the floor. Then return to a standing position.
- Move as quickly as possible through a complete range of motion while maintaining good form.
- Increase the weight for each set, or as you are able, while maintaining or increasing the number of reps.

BACK ROLL TUCK JUMPS

| Week 9: 10 reps |
| Week 10: 8 reps |
| Week 11: 6 reps |

Begin in a standing position, feet hip-width apart.

Drop your butt to your heels.

Using your legs for momentum, roll onto your back, extending your legs straight until they are slightly past your head.

Rock forward onto your feet, keeping your butt down, near your heels. Don't stand up.

Jump straight up as high as you can, hugging your knees to your chest, and release back down. Be sure you bring your knees to your chest, not your chest down to your knees.

Land with your hips above your knees on the balls of your feet, keeping your balance so you can stick your landing.

Return to the start position before repeating.

HIP FLEXOR STRETCH

Pictured on page 161.

SEQUENCE 13

Fire Hydrant/Bridge Walkout Combo

Do 10 times forward, 10 times backward, 10 times side.

Repeat on the opposite leg.

Then do 6-step Bridge Walkouts. Repeat 3 times.

Do 1 set.

Elevated Bulgarian Lunges

Week 9: Max reps for 30 seconds on one side. Repeat on the
other side.

Week 10: Max reps for 20 seconds on one side. Repeat on the
other side.

Week 11: Max reps for 15 seconds on one side. Repeat on the
other side.

Bronco Kick Tuck Jumps

Week 9: Do 10 reps.

Week 10: Do 8 reps.

Week 11: Do 6 reps.

*Alternate sets of Elevated Bulgarian Lunges and Bronco Kick
Tuck Jumps.*

Repeat 3 times.

Hip Flexor Stretch

Do 30 seconds each side.

Do 1 set.

SEQUENCE 13 EXERCISES

FIRE HYDRANT/BRIDGE WALKOUT COMBO

Pictured on pages 154–55.

ELEVATED BULGARIAN LUNGES

Week 9: 30 seconds each side
Week 10: 20 seconds each side
Week 11: 15 seconds each side

- Begin with your front foot on a 1-to-2-inch plate; your front heel is flat on the plate. Your back foot is elevated on a bench, with the ball of your foot resting on the bench.

Your back leg should be as straight as possible. Hold the weights at your sides.

- Lower yourself straight down into a lunge position, without leaning forward, until your knee is bent slightly deeper than 90 degrees.
- Raise back up to the start position.
- Do on one side before repeating on the opposite side.
- Increase the weight for each set, or as you are able, while maintaining or increasing the number of reps.

BRONCO KICK TUCK JUMPS

Week 9: 10 reps
Week 10: 8 reps
Week 11: 6 reps

Begin in a standing position, feet shoulder-width apart.

Reach your hands forward in front of your feet and place your palms flat on the floor. Your knees are bent, butt in the air. Transfer all your weight to the hands.

Kick both feet straight back into the air, as high and fast as possible.

Return to the previous position, landing on your toes, with your knees bent but not touching the floor. Your hand position does not change.

Quickly stand so your knees are in a bent position, hips back, ready for the jump.

Without pausing, jump up to a Tuck Jump for maximum height.

Land with your knees bent; do not drop your hips below your butt.

Return to the start position and repeat.

HIP FLEXOR STRETCH

Pictured on page 161.

SEQUENCE 14

Fire Hydrant/Bridge Walkout Combo

Do 10 times forward, 10 times backward, 10 times side.

Repeat on the opposite leg.

Then do 6-step Bridge Walkouts. Repeat 3 times.

Do 1 set.

Straight-Legged Dead Lifts

Week 9: Max reps for 30 seconds.

Week 10: Max reps for 20 seconds.

Week 11: Max reps for 15 seconds.

Attack Depth Jumps

Week 9: Do 5 reps (18-to-24-inch box).

Week 10: Do 4 reps (24-to-36-inch box).

Week 11: Do 3 reps (36-to-48-inch box).

Alternate sets of Straight-Legged Dead Lifts and Attack Depth Jumps.

Repeat 3 times.

Hip Flexor Stretch

Do 30 seconds each side.

Do 1 set.

SEQUENCE 14 EXERCISES

FIRE HYDRANT/BRIDGE WALKOUT COMBO

Pictured on pages 154–55.

STRAIGHT-LEGGED DEAD LIFTS

Week 9: 30 seconds
Week 10: 20 seconds
Week 11: 15 seconds

Stand with your hips slightly back while holding a barbell in front of your thighs.

- Push your hips back slightly and bend at the hips with your legs straight, back flat, and shoulders back, lowering the weights as close to the floor as possible until they are over your feet, without losing form.
- Quickly return to a standing position and repeat. Remember, in this phase you're working for speed, so these are quick reps.
- Increase the weight for each set, or as you are able, while maintaining or increasing the number of reps.

ATTACK DEPTH JUMPS

Note: This is a rapid-fire set of moves; don't pause between steps. If you have to take a moment to position yourself for the next step, work to do the steps more smoothly as you progress.

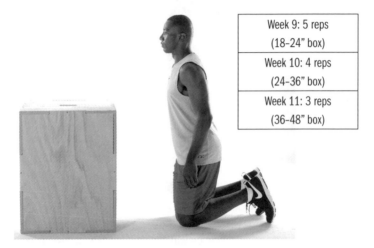

| Week 9: 5 reps (18–24" box) |
| Week 10: 4 reps (24–36" box) |
| Week 11: 3 reps (36–48" box) |

Begin on your knees, with your back tall and straight. Your toes are pointed at the floor.

Lower your butt to your heels.

Dip quickly for momentum, then jump to a squat position. Land on the balls of your feet.

From the squat position, jump onto a box, landing with your knees slightly bent.

Jump forward as high as you can off the box.

Land on the balls of your feet. Don't drop your butt below your hips on landing. After landing, stand straight up.

Turn around to face the box again and drop to your knees. Your toes are pointed at the floor.

Lower your butt to your heels.

Dip quickly for momentum, then jump to squat position. Land on the balls of your feet.

From the squat position jump onto the box, landing with your knees slightly bent. After landing, stand straight up.

Jump forward off the box, landing on the balls of your feet. The jump is not for maximum height. You can just jump to the floor. Don't drop your butt below your hips on landing.

- All the above steps equal 1 rep.
- Turn around again and repeat as quickly as you are able.

HIP FLEXOR STRETCH

Pictured on page 161.

SEQUENCE 15

Fire Hydrant/Bridge Walkout Combo

Do 10 times forward, 10 times backward, 10 times side.

Repeat on the opposite leg.

Then do 6-step Bridge Walkouts. Repeat 3 times.

Do 1 set.

Weighted Calf Raises

Week 9: Max reps for 30 seconds.

Week 10: Max reps for 20 seconds.

Week 11: Max reps for 15 seconds.

Do 3 sets.

Calf Stretch

Do 30 seconds each side.

Do 1 set.

SEQUENCE 15 EXERCISES

FIRE HYDRANT/BRIDGE WALKOUT COMBO

Pictured on pages 154–55.

WEIGHTED CALF RAISES

| Week 9: 30 seconds |
| Week 10: 20 seconds |
| Week 11: 15 seconds |

Stand with your toes on a plate, heels on the floor, barbell resting behind your neck on your shoulders.

Explode up onto your toes for maximum height, and continue raising and lowering your heels as quickly as possible for maximum reps in the allotted time, keeping good form.

CALF STRETCH

30 seconds each side

- Without weights, stand with one foot on a plate (at least 4 inches off the floor), heel over the edge.
- Slowly lower your heel off the plate until you feel a stretch in your calf. Hold without pulsing or bouncing.
- Switch legs and repeat.

PHASE 3: *FLIGHT*

EXPLOSIVE TOTAL BODY

Day 2 and Day 5

Weeks 9, 10, and 11: Maximum reps of each exercise for 30 seconds. Work to increase reps each week.

Clap Push-ups

Pull-up/Chin-up Release Combo
Alternate sets of each. Repeat 3 times.

Clean to Overhead Press

Bicep Curl
Alternate sets of each. Repeat 3 times.

Elevated Pike Push-ups

Alternating Frog Plank
Alternate sets of each. Repeat 3 times.

Power Side Plank

EXPLOSIVE TOTAL BODY EXERCISES

CLAP PUSH-UPS

Weeks 9, 10, 11:
30 seconds

Begin in a plank position with your abs tight, back straight, hands directly under your shoulders. Stand on your toes. Bend your elbows to the side.

Lower your chest 1 inch from the floor into a push-up.

- Using your hips and entire upper body, explode up so the hands are off the floor and your hands clap before returning them to the floor. Repeat immediately for the specified time.
- You may want to put a mat under your hands to cushion your landing.

PULL-UP/CHIN-UP RELEASE COMBO

Weeks 9, 10, 11:
30 seconds

Begin hanging from a sturdy pull-up bar, hands slightly wider than shoulder-width apart, palms facing away from you, knees slightly bent.

Pull yourself up until your chin is above the bar, using your legs, hips, and entire upper body for momentum.

When your chin is above the bar, quickly release and switch hands so your palms are now facing you; this is the chin-up position. Lower yourself until your arms are fully extended.

- Now pull yourself up again into a chin-up, so your chin is over the bar.
- Then release your hands again to switch into a pull-up position and repeat the entire exercise, switching hands each time.
- Each time you reach the top, you release, reverse your hands, lower yourself, and raise back up again.
- This is a very advanced move I do with my pros; it requires a great deal of overall explosiveness and hand speed. Use a spotter if you feel you may need extra help.

CLEAN TO OVERHEAD PRESS

You may use a barbell or dumbbells for this exercise.

Weeks 9, 10, 11:
30 seconds

Begin with the bar at your thighs, hips back, knees slightly bent. Your hands are slightly more than shoulder-width apart.

Raise the bar until your elbows are at 90 degrees to the sides, then
snap your elbows down and forward so the bar comes up in front of
your shoulders.

Throw your hips back and bend your knees for momentum, then quickly explode up into an overhead press, lifting the bar straight overhead.

- Reverse the steps and return to the start.
- Increase the weight for each set, or as you are able, while maintaining or increasing the number of reps.

BICEP CURL

Weeks 9, 10, 11:
30 seconds

Hold dumbbells at your sides, wrists straight and turned forward so your palms are facing away from you. Raise the dumbbells straight up to your shoulders. Your elbows do not move forward or back.

- Do as many reps as possible in the specified time, keeping your form.
- Increase the weight for each set, or as you are able, while maintaining or increasing the number of reps.

ELEVATED PIKE PUSH-UPS

Weeks 9, 10, 11:
30 seconds

Begin with your feet on a box or bench, hands flat on the floor, with fingers pointing straight ahead, legs straight as possible, butt up in the air. Glutes stay tight.

- Lower your head toward the floor (but not touching the floor) as you bend your elbows outward. Then push yourself back up again. Repeat.
- If you feel you might tumble forward, you can place a cushion or mat in front of you. If you feel you need extra support, use a spotter to help pull you up from the hips.

ALTERNATING FROG PLANK

Weeks 9, 10, 11:
30 seconds

Begin in a hand plank position on your toes, abs and glutes tight, back straight.

- Bring one knee up and cross it under your body to the opposite elbow. Your outer thigh is parallel to the floor, with your toes pointed. Don't allow your thigh to drop to the floor; keep it elevated as your reach your knee as far as possible.
- Alternate legs for maximum reps.

POWER SIDE PLANK

Weeks 9, 10, 11:
30 seconds

Begin in a side plank position on one hand, opposite arm overhead, abs and glutes tight, back straight. Bend your top knee toward your chest. Don't allow your hips to sink toward the floor.

- Then rotate your torso (keeping the leg elevated and knee bent) until your shoulders are square to the floor and your arm is fully extended under your chest.
- Return to the starting side plank position and repeat for maximum reps on each side.

PHASE 3: *FLIGHT*

Rest and Recovery
Days 3, 6, and 7, and all of Week 12

Even though Week 12 is at the end of the program, you should still take the week to fully recover before you begin weight training again. If you're planning to repeat Jump Attack, take two weeks off before beginning again (see chapter 10, "The Maintenance Phase," for further discussion).

The Rest and Recovery Days are essential for helping your body repair and adapt to new challenges; rest days are as important to your success as the days you're working out. This is when your body gets stronger. You don't actually build new muscle in the gym; that's where you tear it down. The new muscle is built while you rest and heal from an intense workout. No rest means no healing, which means no new muscle.

And you definitely can't get your best results if you're too fatigued to give your best effort; tired muscles are ineffective muscles. So no weight training during the Rest and Recovery Days. Continue to use your body: play your sport, stay active, but allow your muscles to heal. See chapter 8, on rest, recovery, and injuries, for further discussion.

CHAPTER 7

JUMP ATTACK FUEL

B e honest: When it comes to eating and drinking, what are you willing to give up to get where you want to be?

I can't count how many athletes have said to me, "I'll do anything to play, I want to be the best, just tell me what I have to do!" Then I tell them to give up bacon double cheeseburgers and soda, and their hair starts to fall out.

When a player tells me he's "hungry," I sometimes have to wonder if he's hungry for success or for dessert.

When you make the commitment to become a serious athlete, your priority must become eating for physical excellence, no matter how much you love fries. If you're working to get stronger and build your body, you have to eat in a way that supports muscle growth and recovery and gives you energy when you need it. You're eating for athleticism now, not for entertainment. I'm not telling you to sacrifice taste or good food, but if you're serious about your body and how it performs, you have to take care of the machinery. Think of yourself as a race car: without the right fuel, you're not going very far or very fast.

Not the first time you've heard this, right? Most athletes know the way they eat has everything to do with the way they play; there's nothing new about that. So then explain this to me: Why, after committing to endless hours of training and practice and competition, is it so difficult to commit to a healthy and effective diet? How is it possible to spend hours in the gym, sweating and working and swearing you'll do anything to be the best, and then sabotage it all with what you're putting into your body? Why is it so hard for so many athletes to eat right?

Here's why: Because they think good nutrition is too complicated. What should I eat? When should I eat it? How much should I eat? It's too expensive! I don't cook!

A lot of athletes believe nutrition is all or nothing; you eat right or you don't. And then when some expert or trainer tells you what to do, you get a giant list of everything you shouldn't eat, and suddenly you feel like you just lost your best friend. You hear over and over what's "bad" for you, and you feel guilty for eating it. You don't have the time or desire to mess around in the kitchen or grocery store. You need something fast and easy.

I believe in keeping it simple. When I have a player who needs to change his eating habits, I'm going to give him a program he can handle, because if it's too restrictive and overwhelming, he's going to quit. I have to be realistic about food and alcohol and other things that they're just not going to give up, so I give my guys choices. I know I can't get the younger ones to give up fast food; they live on it. You know why it's called fast food? Because it speeds you to the end of your career. Okay, you don't want to eliminate it? Then you have to make smarter choices. If you want the burger, cut the fries. Choose chicken sandwiches instead of cheeseburgers. If you must have a cheeseburger, instead of twice a day, have it once. When you get that bacon double cheeseburger with the three slices of bread, toss one slice of bread and half the bacon. Then eventually throw two slices of bread away and a little more bacon. Instead of drinking two sodas, how about one soda and one bottle of water? Or get totally crazy and give up soda for good? I know you can't stand egg-white omelets. How about two whites and one whole egg?

I give my guys eating guidelines, a yes/no list of foods. I'm not giving them a meal-by-meal diet, with how many ounces of chicken they can eat and how many blueberries are allowed. Everyone is going to cheat on a diet. Everyone. And as soon as they cheat, they think it's over because they cheated. I don't want to see you measuring a quarter cup of cheese, I want you to use common sense. You don't need a degree in nutrition to know it's better to eat grilled chicken than a bag of chips, or that it's healthier to eat fruit than candy bars. The question is: Do you have a strong enough desire and backbone to control your eating, or does eating control you? You can't get to where you want to be unless you're willing to do what you need to do. The key to success is the willingness to give up what's preventing you from getting there.

That doesn't mean you have to do everything at once. You're kidding yourself if you think you can drastically change your diet overnight; it usually works for a couple of days, and then it becomes too difficult. When you change too much too fast, you don't stay with it. Small changes for big results.

Make the transition slowly. Go in stages, gradually introducing changes into your diet. I want you to identify one thing you can give up and eliminate it. Soda, fries, chips, ice cream . . . whatever you feel you can get rid of. After a week, cut something else. Find one thing you can improve on—late-night eating, skipping breakfast— and make that change. Find small ways to improve; they all add up. You will feel so much better, your performance will show it, and before too long, the small changes become a way of life.

And please don't tell me you can eat anything you want and still play great. If you're eating junk and playing well, think about how much better you'd be playing on a good diet. The race car will drive just fine on regular fuel, but give it something special and it performs like never before.

Here are some easy ways to get control of your eating; the more of these you can do, the better you'll perform. Every one of these suggestions will improve your athletic performance in some way. And like all my lists, they're all labeled #1 because they're all equally important.

If you can handle the hard work and training that go into playing your sport, you can handle these basic lifestyle changes. And honestly, if you find you can't follow these few easy guidelines, I think you have to question whether you're serious about achieving your athletic goals. Yes, I know it might be tough to reduce sugar in your diet or give up late-night pizza, but as I tell my clients: You don't have to love the work, you just have to crave the result.

1. Eat five times a day. As an athlete, you need constant energy, not the highs and lows of being on the starving/ stuffed/starving/stuffed roller coaster. That means keeping your hunger in check and your blood sugar consistent so you don't get cravings for snacks and binge on whatever's in front of you. You know what comes after that: the inevitable crash that sends you back for more snacks. Quality food gets quality results. Plan your eating the way you plan your workouts and stick to the schedule. Here's an example of a five-meal day, with some suggestions for what to eat:

- Breakfast (hot cereal such as oatmeal).
- Protein shake or small snack (*Yes*: a small piece of chicken, green apple, handful of nuts. *No*: a doughnut, pretzel, frozen pizza, or candy bar.)
- Lunch (A light meal of carbs and protein, such as a salad or wrap with grilled chicken, something that won't weigh you down for the rest of the afternoon and make you want to nap. If you only have access to fast food, have a chicken sandwich and skip the fries.)
- Protein shake or small snack—whichever you didn't have late in the morning (This is the time of day when most people feel their blood sugar dropping, which gives you that late-afternoon drowsiness. Eating small meals all day should fix that, but if you do feel sluggish, don't reach for candy or other empty calories. Protein digests slower and keeps you feeling full longer.)
- Dinner (protein—chicken/fish/turkey—and green vegetables)

1. Drink a big glass of water before and during every meal. This has two major impacts on your eating. Water will make you feel fuller so you don't overeat. Water also hydrates you. You don't need the calories or sugars in sodas and sports drinks before, during, or after meals; they can actually make you thirstier and they'll make you crave more sugar. Your body is 60 to 70 percent water. Keep it that way.

1. Get your carbs early in the day. Do you put gas in the tank before you drive the car, or when you're on the side of the road waiting for a tow truck? Start your morning with carbs so you can run on the fuel they give you throughout the day. As evening approaches and you become less active, decrease your carb intake and increase your protein (which provides the building blocks for your new muscle). Don't consume more carbs than you can burn; you'll store the calories you don't use, which will eventually make you fat and slow. And most important, get your carbs from whole grain, fruits, and vegetables, not from candy, chips, and soda.

1. Oatmeal for breakfast. Don't tell me you don't have time for breakfast. Make time for it like you make time for practice and workouts and games. It's just as important to your athletic life as everything else you do for your sport. A hot cereal such as plain oatmeal is a great source of complex carbohydrates; it gives you energy and keeps you feeling full all morning. And unlike sugar cereals with little marshmallows and candy-coated fake fruit, it won't give you a sugar high that leaves you feeling low in an hour and dealing with cravings all day. I'm not talking about sweetened flavored oatmeal in the package; you're having plain oatmeal. If you have to add a little skim milk or berries or a drop of peanut butter to it, go ahead, but remember we're cutting your sugars, not slathering them over otherwise healthy food. I know a lot of people like to dress oatmeal up with whipped cream, brown sugar, fruit, or other sweeteners. Don't. We're training for the end result.

1. Choose whole grain, not white or wheat. White or wheat? This is the greatest trick question in the history of processed food. Ask yourself this: If the brown bread is wheat, what's the white bread made from? That's right . . . *wheat*. One is colored brown, the other is bleached white. Same identical wheat. They have nothing to do with what you need: 100 percent whole wheat or 100 percent whole grain. I know you might not always have a choice, but when you do, know the difference between the bread that imitates sugar once it gets into your bloodstream and the bread that fuels your body. Don't be tricked by multigrain—which sounds good but just combines a lot of stuff you don't really want or need with a little bit of whole grain—or "contains whole wheat," which means you're getting some but not enough. When you have a choice, choose whole grain.

And by the way, if you can eliminate bread altogether, that's fine too. There are plenty of other good sources for carbohydrates.

1. Pay attention to portion control. We were all raised to finish everything on our plates, not to waste food. But when you're eating for athletic fuel, you have to know when enough is enough. Just because you're eating something healthy doesn't mean you should consume so much that you feel sick. If you're following the "Eat five times a day" plan, you should never feel so hungry that you have to pig out. When you sit down to eat, remember it's not your last meal; you're going to eat again in a couple of hours. Common sense: Eat to not feel hungry, don't eat to feel stuffed. Thanksgiving only comes once a year; the other 364 days should be about self-control and eating smart.

1. Include greens as often as possible. Low in calories and sugar, high in nutrients, green vegetables give you all of the good and none of the bad. Why greens and not all vegetables? Because other colors have more sugar. Carrots and sweet potatoes have nutritional benefits but they're also higher in sugar. You can include them with your meals, but your emphasis should be loading up on the greens: broccoli, spinach, green beans, lettuce, asparagus.

1. When you just need a snack. It happens. You're not a machine. Sometimes you just have to eat. When you want a snack (in addition to your five scheduled meals), have a green apple; green apples are higher in fiber and aren't as sweet as the reds. Why an apple? When you're done, you're done. You sit down with a bowl of cherries or grapes or nuts, you'll keep putting your hand back in the bowl until you're so stuffed you can't move. It's the same with other small items; a couple turns into a handful, which turns into way more than a snack. When in doubt, go with one apple. It's guaranteed to fill you up until your next meal.

1. Once every two weeks, forget the rules. Just as you take days off from your training, you should take time off from your eating plan and enjoy yourself. I'm not saying go completely crazy with your eating, but it's actually good for your body to get out of your routine and shock the metabolism; it elevates your ability to burn more calories when you give your metabolism extra work to do. And it's good to occasionally set aside the pressure of having to constantly focus on training; you have a better chance of sticking with good eating habits if you can relax the rules once in a while. If there's a holiday or birthday or party, enjoy it. Just remember, the key word is enjoy; don't go wild. You're working too hard the rest of the week to undo it all.

1. If your goal is to lose weight . . . don't eat after 8:00 p.m.
Unless you work out or have a game at night, you don't need any more calories or carbs after dinner; they'll just sit in your body stored as unused fuel, which ultimately turns into fat when it doesn't get used. If you're waking up still full from the night before, you're definitely eating too much too late. Eat just enough in the evening to get you to the morning; you should wake up feeling hungry and ready to go again. If you're really hungry and need to eat, make it lean protein (chicken or turkey breast, for example) and a big glass of water, not sweets or chips with a soda.

1. If your goal is to gain weight . . . eating in the middle of the night is not the way to do it. A full stomach interferes with your ability to get complete rest, and you need that rest. You can have a peanut butter and jelly sandwich (remember to choose whole grain bread) with a big glass of milk at bedtime if you want to add calories; just don't fill yourself with cookies and pretzels. Your best bet is to add weight in the weight room, not with late-night snacks.

I want you to follow all these guidelines, but if I had to stress one point, one thing you can do to improve overall performance, it's this: control your sugar intake, and learn to understand how much sugar is contained in what you eat and drink. This isn't just about cutting calories, although I do want you to control your weight. This is about how your sugar intake affects your performance. I want your energy and blood sugar levels to be steady, without the peaks and valleys, so you can function at a peak level for a longer time. Get rid of the highs and lows, the crashes, the sudden fatigue, so you're not chasing them with more sugar. Control what you consume; don't let it control you.

You might believe that athletes at the pro level have this under control. Not necessarily true. As a rule, I want all my guys to decrease their sugar intake; when I start working with them, they rarely realize how much they consume. If you grew up on soda and juice and candy and chips, that's all your body knows; you have no idea how good you'd feel or how much better you'd play without all that sugar in your system. Once you've developed those bad eating habits, they're extremely hard to break.

I once had a client who couldn't drop weight no matter what he did, no matter how hard I worked him out. I talked to him about his eating. I even hired a cook to make his meals. He still couldn't drop a pound. Finally I went over to his house to talk to his wife, to find out what was going on. I had her make a list of everything he was consuming.

And there it was: two gallons of orange juice every day.

That's a couple thousand calories and more than 300 grams of sugar, before he'd even eaten one forkful of food.

He was shocked to learn that OJ was on the "no" list, because like a lot of people, he was raised to believe that orange juice was "good" for you. And yes, it has its benefits—lots of vitamin C—but you can't drink it by the gallon and expect to lose weight. He had no idea how much sugar he was consuming because his body was completely accustomed to it, and constantly craved more; the more he drank, the more he had to drink. Sugar has a druglike effect on your body, and like any drug, it can easily cause you to become addicted.

If you don't believe me, ask anyone who has been on the diet program I call "The List." This is the program I give to athletes who want to drop weight quickly and safely—twenty-one days of relentless fat loss. The List is a complete menu of foods you can eat and foods you can't eat. If you want to know how much sugar flows through your body, flush it all out for twenty-one days and see how it feels. You have no idea how deeply sugar affects you until you take it all away; the side effects can be intense. You'll get a crazy headache behind one eye. You'll get hot, you'll get cold, you'll want to throw up. You'll shake like a heroin addict going through withdrawal because, guess what? You are. It's a serious challenge. But the results are almost immediate, and it works like nothing else to burn off the fat, reset your sugar levels to where they should be, and boost your performance in every way. I'm not trying to make it easy, I'm making it effective.

I've done it. All my trainers have to do it. So we know if you're cheating.

I'll have a guy come in, supposedly on The List, and he looks just great. Happy, energetic, ready to work. I ask him: "How's the diet?"

"Great!" he says. "No problem!"

I wait a couple days and ask again. "You feeling good?"

"Yep, feeling fine."

"You sticking to the diet?"

"Oh, yeah, I'm good."

Okay, you're not good, you're a liar. Get serious or find another place to fail.

I had a client who wanted (and needed) The List, but I knew once he started, he'd stop training; the low level of carbs can temporarily affect your physical endurance if you're accustomed to performing at a very high level.

"Just show up," I told him. "I don't care what you do once you're here, but I want to see you here."

And he did. On the third day, he dragged himself into the gym, lay down in the middle of the basketball court, and stayed there all day. Never moved. The other guys couldn't use that court.

"You told me to show up," he said with a groan.

The diet will challenge your mental toughness, but when it's done, you've never felt better. Everything is improved, from your endurance and sleep to your skin and mood. You just feel good.

Look, I'm not suggesting you have to live a sugar-free lifestyle to be a great athlete. But it's a fact that the more sugar you consume, the more you'll crave . . . so you'll consume more, and crave more, and . . . well, you get it. If your blood sugar levels are under control, your cravings will be under control too.

In general I find that the guys with more sugar in their diets are the same guys who constantly crave the sports drinks; they need the carbs to replace what they're burning. Athletes with less sugar in their diets are much more content with water; in fact, they won't touch the high-calorie drinks because their bodies don't need them. Players who consume a lot of sugar really feel it when their blood sugar levels drop, while players who are good about keeping sugar out of their diets don't feel that drop.

Now, I have no problem with sports drinks while you're working out, training, practicing hard, as a carbohydrate source to replace what you've burned up and replenish what you've lost. During a game, during a workout, that's the time for this. But not as a beverage while you're sitting around watching TV or having dinner. Way too much sugar. You want to replace sugars you've lost, not add excess to your body. Don't drink your calories. If you want to keep a balance, I have my players alternate one sports drink, one water. Each time-out or break, have whatever you didn't have last time. It's a great way to replenish your carbs while hydrating your body. Remember, your body is 60 to 70 percent water. Give it what it needs.

There are so many products out there for athletes—some of them are terrific, some of them are nonsense—but even the best products can't compensate for an unhealthy diet and lifestyle. If you're eating poorly *and* not getting enough rest *and* consuming alcohol *and* drinking your calories . . . something has to give, and it will be your performance. Addressing the situation with remedies such as sports drinks, energy drinks, caffeine, and alcohol is usually going to create more problems. If you're eating properly, hydrating, and getting your rest, you shouldn't have to rely on artificial means to feeling healthier and more energetic.

Think about it: Why do you reach for an energy drink or caffeine or sugars or snacks? Because you're deficient in something—sleep, nutrition, caloric intake, hydration—and your body is begging for additional "energy." You're tired, sluggish, slow, in need of a boost. Maybe you were up all night on the computer, playing with your phone, definitely not sleeping enough. So you reach for extra help to get you going and stay awake. And when you get that dragging feeling again later in the day, you repeat the process. Terrible habit and an even worse addiction. I have guys who say they just need a quick cup of coffee in the morning to get going. Then they add ten packs of sugar, milk, flavored syrup . . . you might as well eat cake.

I promise you, all those stimulants in energy drinks and caffeinated drinks aren't helping you as an athlete. They throw your heart rate way up, affect your central nervous system and your fine motor movements, alter your mental capacity, get you feeling hyper. And then of course what goes up must come down, so you crash, right in the middle of a game. Whatever boost you had just vaporized. Crash.

Reduce or eliminate the sugar and caffeine and see how good you'll feel and how much better you'll perform. What do you want more: the results or the doughnut?

And finally, a few words about alcohol. Plain and simple, all your hard work and training are erased by alcohol consumption. You've heard of alcohol poisoning? What does that tell you? In large quantities, it's a poison. Even in small amounts, it slows your reaction time, decreases your coordination and balance, causes you to fatigue much faster, and affects just about every element of your performance. Not just while the alcohol is in your system, but for days after you've consumed it.

I'm always asked if I allow my players to drink. Well, they're grown adults who have to make their own decisions. And they like to relax once in a while; they're no different from anyone else. But it has to be in moderation, and they have to control their drinking; the drinking can't control them.

Bottom line: Longevity and long-term success in athletics is the result of giving your body the opportunity to perform, to improve, to succeed. As players get older, they begin to understand what's at stake, what they have to do to continue performing at a high level. They understand what they have to give up to sustain their bodies and careers.

Believe me: The minute you begin to make good nutrition a priority, you'll have an immediate edge over everyone else. Make them wonder how you did it.

CHAPTER 8

THE TRAINER'S ROOM
REST, RECOVERY, AND INJURIES

I t's not a weakness to recognize your body's need to recover, it's a weakness to be so addicted to training and so scared to miss a day that your body can't keep up with your obsession. A car will go farther on a full tank than on fumes; so will you. The Rest and Recovery Days in this program fill your tank, and allow you to go faster and farther the next day.

Jump Attack has three rest days each week: Days 3, 6, and 7, and one full week of rest at the end of each phase. For this program, rest doesn't mean lying in bed watching TV all day; it means staying active and allowing your body to use its new explosiveness. When I say rest, I mean no weights and no intense training; stay away from the areas you've been working all week. Do a stretch routine, use foam rollers on the areas that are sore and tender, take an ice bath, just mess around or play your sport.

An exception to the "no lying around watching TV" rule: for one rest day per week, shut it down completely. Take a mental break, a day you don't have to think about training or playing or whatever else you usually have to do on the other six days. You will have earned it.

I want you to take that break. It's not an option in this program, it's a necessity. Rest and recovery are an essential part of your training and conditioning; you can't give maximum effort or get maximum results with tired, fatigued muscles. It's not a sign of mental or physical weakness to take days off so your body can heal; I would never allow my clients to work every day without scheduled rest days. Rest is part of your training; it allows your body to recover and adapt so you can keep going and get stronger. Relentless training is not smart training.

I'm not talking about taking a rest day because you woke up late or you were feeling slow so you decided to blow off your workout; that's not a rest day, that's just laziness. I'm talking about planned rest days that are built into your schedule, so you know in advance you won't be working out. Effective training doesn't happen by accident; you have to structure your workouts with careful intention. Jump Attack does the planning for you so you don't have to wonder when to rest. Stick to the schedule and you won't have to think about it.

And if you're one of those people who never takes a day off and you're happy with how you're performing, imagine how much better you'd perform if your body was fully rested and working at 90 to 100 percent capacity instead of maybe 60 to 70 percent. If you're never resting, you're never able to give your best.

Jump Attack is about staying fresh and strong. The workout is designed to maximize explosiveness; the muscles have to be long and strong for that to happen. That's why I want you to follow the program as scheduled: legwork only twice a week. That's it. More is not better. In fact, more is going to set you back. Why? Because we're training your muscles to snap like a rubber band. What happens when you stretch a rubber band too far for too long, snapping it over and over? It starts to wear out, the snap slowly weakens, and the band eventually breaks. Now it's useless.

This program puts so much stress on your muscles, they'll be as useless as the overused rubber band if you don't give them the time they need to recover. Take care of your body with rest, nutrition, ice, and hydration.

Your rest days also give you a mental recharge, a little time to get your mind away from training and the hard work still ahead of you. Even the pros have to take time away from the daily grind, to clear their heads and blow off some steam. When Michael was getting ready for the season, he shut down everything else except his workouts and golf; the golf was to give his mind that mental break so everything wasn't about the workouts. Other guys spend time with their kids and families, manage their business relationships, work on their charities, just something that isn't all about training and athletics. Even if you're completely focused on your sport, you have to think about something else occasionally or you'll go nuts. You can't be strong from the neck down if you're not strong from the neck up, so take the time to clear your head and refocus.

I get many questions from athletes—from kids to pros—about how to handle rest and recovery and how to deal with injuries. Here are some of the more common issues.

MY SCHEDULE IS SO PACKED FROM SPORTS AND SCHOOL AND WORK THAT I DON'T GET A LOT OF SLEEP. DOES IT MATTER?

Sleep is one of the most critical components of training and performance; that's when your body heals and recovers. For your body to work at its maximum ability, you must get your rest. Make it a priority, just like eating right and going to practice; it's as important. Instead of staying up late watching a movie or hanging around the Internet, shut it all down and go to sleep. You will notice the difference almost immediately.

WHAT IF I HAVE GAMES ON REST DAYS?

You can compete or do anything you want on Day 3, Day 6, and Day 7 (Rest and Recovery Days); I just don't want you using weights to work the muscles you've been working. On one of those days, though, you should take a complete day off from everything that requires physical and mental focus on training and playing sports. If you're not sure how to fit Jump Attack around your game schedule, look at the dates you have games, and start your Jump Attack schedule on a day that won't create a conflict between that one rest day and a game. If you have to adjust your workout days slightly, do it, but stay as close to the schedule as possible.

WILL I BE SORE WHILE I'M DOING JUMP ATTACK?

Look at it this way: If you're not working, you won't be sore. If you're doing all the exercises correctly, you'll feel it, and you'll know exactly what you've been working on. So if you have a tough leg workout on Monday, you'll probably still feel it on Thursday during your second leg workout that week. If you didn't work hard enough on Monday, you probably *won't* feel it Thursday. We're training your body in ways it probably hasn't been worked, and that brings temporary soreness. The key word is temporary. Don't quit just because you feel the results of a hard workout; that would be like dropping a class because the first day was tough. You have to go back and work through it.

During each phase, the soreness will decrease. But be warned: When you move to a new phase, you may experience increased soreness again as your body experiences something new, including short-term discomfort in the hip area and the other muscles we're working, maybe a burning sensation in the legs, but that's normal. You'll get over it. If you experience something beyond soreness, such as actual pain, you should check with your doctor right away.

WHAT'S THE FASTEST WAY TO GET RID OF MUSCLE SORENESS?

Move. The more you use your muscles, the faster they'll start to flush out the lactic acid burn you get from really working them in a new way (and there's a lot of that in this program). The worst thing you can do for tired, sore muscles is sit and moan about the soreness; it will take you so much longer to feel better. Use your body. Stretch. Stay hydrated. And, as always, get comfortable being uncomfortable. As soon as you accept that great results require some discomfort, you'll stop thinking about how it feels and you'll start focusing on those results. When you want the outcome more than you care about the soreness, the momentary discomfort won't seem like such a big deal.

HOW DO I KNOW IF I'M INJURED OR JUST HURT?

If you're doing the exercises in this program correctly and you're getting a proper warm-up, cool down, and recovery, your body might occasionally be hurting, but chances are minimal that you will become injured.

There's a big difference between hurt and injured. Hurt means you're uncomfortable but you can work through it. Injured means you should stop and get medical attention.

When you're hurt, you might be experiencing stiffness, soreness, burning in the muscle . . . you can work through those things. Stretch, and use a foam roller on the sore spots. Doing the workout might make you feel better because you'll be using the muscles to flush out some of the soreness. It's okay to feel achy and sore; it's a sign you really did something. But if you really can't go, take a day or two off and see if you feel better.

If you still can't work through it, or if you're feeling something painful in a joint, or a sharp, pulling pain in a muscle, you may have an injury. If that's the case, see your team trainer or your doctor immediately. The sooner you get the right medical attention, the sooner you can start to heal and get back to work.

Depending on the problem, you can frequently get effective relief from RICE until you can see a doctor:

- Rest
- Ice
- Compression
- Elevation

Get the affected area wrapped, get some ice on it, and elevate it.

WHAT'S THE BENEFIT OF ICE BATHS?

There is no better way to bring down inflammation and speed recovery than an ice bath. I've used them for my clients all the way back to

MJ, simply because they work quickly and effectively. After intensely hard work, ice baths are the best way to get yourself back into the gym the next day, performing at maximum capacity for maximum results.

When people question the necessity of sitting in a tub of ice, I tell them this: Why do we keep food in a refrigerator? When you keep things cold, they last longer and stay fresh. What happens when you leave meat at room temperature? It spoils. Milk, cheese, eggs . . . they all rot if you don't keep them cool. It's the same for your body. Heat is not your friend. Your body even comes with its own cooling system: sweating. What happens when you have a fever or you get overheated? You feel sick and exhausted. What's the main reason people can't get through a workout? They get hot, then tired, then they have to stop; their core temperatures get too high, they're already too warm from warming up. And when something gets too warm, it has to cool down. Your muscles and joints are no different from the rest of your body; when they get inflamed, ice is the answer.

Is it comfortable to sit in ice? No. Is it the best thing for inflammation and soreness? Absolutely. Do you need to be comfortable or do you need fast results?

It's easy: once a day, ten to fifteen minutes max. That's it. Waist high; do not submerge the chest or head. If possible, do it within an hour or so after a workout or game, but if you can't do it that soon, do it when you can. You can take an ice bath every day, and you will benefit more from a recovery standpoint than anything else you do. If ice isn't available, you can use cold water in a tub; it doesn't have to be filled with ice.

WHEN SHOULD I USE HEAT INSTEAD OF ICE?

In general, I prefer you don't use heat unless you've been told by a trainer or doctor to do so; heat on an inflammation will make it worse. Of course, warmth feels better on the body than cold, so people tend to look for reasons to use heat. But in most cases, ice will do the trick. There are times when heat is beneficial, such as when your muscles and joints are so sore and stiff that you can't work out, and heat is the only thing that makes you feel looser and more comfortable. But many times, a good basic warm-up will give you the same result.

CHAPTER 9

THE RESULTS

There's only one reason you're doing this program: *results*. Everything you do, everything you work for has to be for the end result, or why else would you do it?

But getting the end result in explosiveness is tricky, because how do you know when you've reached the end? You push a little more, a little more, you think you can go a little higher, a little faster . . . there's not really a finish line. It's not like you can "win" at explosiveness.

So how do you know if you've succeeded at Jump Attack?

We're looking for improvement.

Quicker, higher, faster, stronger, longer . . . you can continue to improve in so many ways, long before you reach the final result. I know everyone is craving that big increase in their vertical jump, but if that's all you want, you're really cheating the rest of your game.

This program will get you closer to your goal than you were before. Results completely vary from person to person—some will get maximum results doing it once, some will get better results the second or third time. A lot will depend on how aggressively you attack the workout, and whether you show up on schedule and give it your maximum effort. Genetics also have something to do with it, but with commitment and relentless mental and physical drive, you can maximize the gifts you were born with.

The best way to get results? Do the exercises as described and use good form. If you're struggling to complete an exercise, you're either going too fast, using too much weight, or you're not using the correct form. Anytime someone says they're not getting results from this workout, it's usually because they get caught up in the number of reps they can do in thirty seconds, or they add too much weight to the bar, and they lose their form. If you can squat 135 perfectly, but you decide to make things interesting by throwing 225 on the bar to see how heavy you can lift, most likely you'll struggle and you'll have terrible form. And all you achieved was sabotaging your results.

It's possible you may only be able to increase two to three reps throughout the entire program. Don't be surprised if that's the case. It's perfectly normal. I'd be more concerned if you increased from one rep to ten, because if you're increasing that much, you either didn't do enough when you started or you're not doing the exercises right. We're looking for gradual improvement. Everyone will improve at a different rate, depending on your body and build and genetics. Just know that if you do the program correctly, you will definitely improve.

As I said earlier, I don't measure vertical jumps for my clients; I don't consider it a measurement of skill or ability. It doesn't tell me how fast you are, how quickly you can explode in different directions, or how high you bounce up on your second or third jump. And it certainly doesn't measure commitment or determination or heart. I don't care what you can do in the gym when there's no opponent and no pressure; I want to see what you can do during a game. I want to see how you play.

If a guy really needs to measure his progress and see how he's doing, I'll ask him in the beginning of the program to show me a dunk he can't do. I'll have him try two or three times, and tell him to remember how far he was from dunking. Then after six to eight weeks, I'll say, "Remember that dunk you couldn't do? Go try again." I know he's going to be shocked by the difference; they always are. That's how I want you to measure improvement, by testing your ability as an athlete, not by jumping up once to touch the wall.

However, I know a lot of you want that vertical jump measurement to chart your gains, so I'm giving you the guidelines for testing during the Jump Attack program. Remember, this test is optional and reflects only a small part of the gains you might experience during the program.

Test on Day 1 before you begin Jump Attack, and test again on Day 90 (or five to seven days after you do the last leg workout). I want you to wait those five to seven days at the end so your legs are fully rested, allowing you to get the maximum height on your vertical jump.

Resist testing yourself in the middle of the ninety-day program; you may actually see a decline in your measurement because your muscles will likely be tired; they'll still be developing and still learning what they're supposed to do.

- There is no right answer to this test, and no specific measurement that defines success. We're looking for improvement, not a specific number. If you've improved, that's success.
- You will know your true results when you're playing or practicing your sport, and you realize what you're able to do that you weren't able to do before.
- You may not reach your maximum jumping height within the first ninety days; you will likely increase your jump if you go through the program a second or third time. Even-

tually you'll reach your maximum jump, but you can continue to gain in other areas by continuing the program.

THE VERTICAL JUMP TEST

There are several ways to do the test; if you have access to equipment designed for this or you prefer another method of testing, feel free to do it your own way. This is an easy way to test yourself at home.

- With chalk on your longest finger, stand sideways next to a wall.
- Stand straight and tall, reach up as high as you can, and tap the wall, leaving a mark with the chalk. That's your first measurement.
- For your next measurement, you may have to move slightly away from the wall to give yourself room to jump.

Standing in the same location, prepare to jump with a quick dip for momentum, without hesitation before you jump. Your feet do not move until the jump; there are no intermediate steps.

Jump up as high as you can, tapping the wall again and leaving a second mark with the chalk. That is your second measurement.

- The difference between the two chalk marks is your vertical jump measurement.

Give yourself three tries to repeat the jump; you may not get the same number each time. Take the highest measurement of the three jumps. You do not have to repeat the first standing tap. That measurement will not change.

Record your vertical jump measurement. Remember, in the end, all that matters is how you play.

Day 1 Vertical Jump

_____

_____

_____

Day 90 Vertical Jump

_____

_____

_____

CHAPTER 10

THE MAINTENANCE PHASE

So after you've completed the ninety-day Jump Attack program . . . then what?

You've done everything from Bronco Tuck Jumps to Burpee Dead Lifts to Lunge Buttkickers, and want to keep going, just to see how high you can take it. You got a taste of how it feels to explode into the air with power and athleticism. You achieved success in a program so advanced, challenging, and effective that elite athletes all over the world come back to do it again and again.

What's next?

Get ready for more and do it again.

Look, excellence isn't about what you can do in ninety days; the greats never stop working to improve, and neither should you. If you're really serious about getting results, if you're never satisfied because you know you can do more, then continue what you started here and keep pushing yourself.

You need reasons to repeat the program? Here are a few:

- You're asking yourself to improve on the hardest thing to improve: explosiveness. It's possible that it might take longer than ninety days for you to reach your full potential.

- Explosiveness isn't a permanent condition. Your body needs continuous training to stay that way. Keep working to maintain everything you've gained, and achieve even greater gains.
- You never know how high you can go.
- Plain and simple, it's a great workout, guaranteed to make you a better athlete if you commit to doing the work.

Don't be surprised if you see greater results the second time around, as your body becomes accustomed to its new athletic ability. Most people will reach their maximum gains after doing the program two or three times. And when I talk about gains, I mean in all-around athleticism, not just your vertical jump. Can you do something you couldn't do before? That's the true test for measuring your success each time you do this program.

If you've finished Jump Attack and want to do it again:

- Let your body fully recover before beginning again. A fresh start with strong, healthy muscles will allow you to give your maximum effort, which in turn will give you maximum results.
- Wait at least two weeks from last leg workout before starting again. Take more time if you feel your body needs it. You'll know when you're ready to start again.
- Stay active during the downtime between completing the program and repeating it. Play your sport, work out, show your new muscles what they're supposed to be doing, but

stay away from heavy weights and intense training. Go back to the workout regimen you were doing before Jump Attack and see how much more strength and endurance you have.

- When you're ready to begin the program again, start at the beginning and do everything the same, except for the following changes:

  1. In Phase 1, the "hold" times increase from 60–90–120 seconds to 90–120–180, because your body is now better prepared for longer challenges. If you're repeating the program more than twice, stay at these times.

  2. For exercises using weights, use the same amount of weight you were using at the end of the program, and increase from there. Do not go back to the lighter weights you used at the beginning of the last program; you're ready for more.

  3. Everything else stays the same. The program is the program. Keep doing it as scheduled, giving maximum effort for maximum results.

If you never worked on your jumping skills before you did Jump Attack, you will probably benefit from repeating the program because you likely have more room to improve. Ninety days aren't enough to show what you're truly capable of achieving.

If you're an experienced athlete who trains on a regular basis and you've spent a lot of time training to be explosive, you will still probably benefit from repeating the program. Just keep in mind that the more you improve, the less room you'll likely have to improve further. After you've achieved certain gains, it's physically impossible to continually increase your jumping ability, or everyone would be bouncing through the roof. Your body does have limitations, even with the best training. If you did the program once and gained six inches in your vertical, you may not gain another six inches if you do it again. It's possible, but at some point you'll reach your limit. Even the fastest runner in the world can't shave ten seconds off his time just by training more. Eventually you're going to hit your plateau. You can bump up that ceiling slightly, but generally at some point you will reach your maximum benefits.

And even if you've reached your maximum jump, you can—and will—still see improvements in other areas. Even the best never stop finding ways to get better.

Yes, it's hard, and it's a major commitment that most people can't ever understand. But you have to feel the darkness before you see the light. Maybe you're just beginning to see that light.

If you stop doing the work, if you think you've done enough and you can slow down your training, understand that all the improvements you've made will begin to decline . . . which is why my clients continually train with the exercises in this program, and use the sequences as the basis for their regular workouts.

And if you got the results you were seeking . . . that's actually the main reason to continue. Do it to maintain what you worked for, do it to stay at the top of your game and to push the top even higher. Michael was already "Air Jordan" when he started this program, but he worked at it relentlessly because he always wanted to stay at the top and go even higher.

Take that mind-set with you into your training, your goals, your life, and see how high you can fly.

INDEX

squats, 15, 21, 38, 45, 50, 58, 162, 163–64
stamina, 65–66
static stretching, 24–25
Straight-Legged Dead Lift Hold, 82, 83–84
Straight-Legged Dead Lift Pump, 82, 85
Straight-Legged Dead Lifts, 124, 125–27, 177, 178–79
strength, 7, 23, 28, 148, 229, 239
stretching:
    Explosive Sequences and, 47–48
    Jump Attack formula and, 14, 16, 18, 20, 23–24
    during Phase 1, 67
    during Phase 2, 101
    during Phase 3, 149
    soreness and, 225
    warm-up routine and, 54, 57
    when and how to stretch, 5
    see also specific stretches
sugar reduction, 210, 211, 212, 213, 215–20
supersets, 102, 150
sweating, 227
swimming, 50

teams, 10, 55
technique, 49, 58
temperature, 54, 227
tennis, 54, 55
time commitment, 45–46, 53, 55
Tiptoe Squat Hold, 71, 73
Tiptoe Squat Pump, 71, 74
Total Body workouts, 48, 54–55, 57, 68
    Explosive, 191–204
    Power, 134–45
    Relentless, 89–97
    see also core; lower body; upper body
trainers, personal, 37, 49, 221–28

training, 5, 9, 11, 12, 33, 37, 58
    body vs. sport, 61
    details and, 27–28, 67, 101, 149
    evolution of, 4–5, 15–16
    for maximum results, 67–69, 101–3, 149–51
    resistance, 3
    rules for relentless, 29–43
    smart vs. hard, 40–42
    teaching vs., 27
Tricep Push-up Hold, 89, 95
Tuck Jumps, 15, 52, 113, 116–17

uncomfortableness, 7, 33–34, 52, 66, 225
undertraining, 58
upper body, 5–6, 25, 35, 46, 54–57, 65

V-Calf Stretch, 86, 88
vegetables, green, 213–14
vertical jumps, 9, 10, 11, 12, 59, 230, 238
vertical jump test, 11, 60, 61, 231–35
volleyball, 54
V-Up Hold, 86, 87
V-Up Pump, 86, 88

Wade, Dwyane, 2, 5, 15, 33
walking, 38
warm-up routine, 53–54, 225
water, 211, 215, 218
Weighted Calf Raises, 130, 131–32, 187, 188–89
weight loss, 7, 27, 52, 215
weights, 18, 21, 23, 53, 99, 102, 149, 239
weight training, 7, 16, 23, 25, 41, 49
whole grains, 212–13, 215
willingness, 29, 39, 209
working hard, 31, 32, 98
workout program, stages of, 33, 34, 35–36, 37, 63

workout schedule, 3–4, 5, 70, 104, 152
    game day and, 57–58
    interruptions in, 56
    off-season and, 57
    for Phase 1, 70
    for Phase 2, 104
    for Phase 3, 152
    rest days and, 59, 222
    sticking to the, 17–18, 24, 31
    time required for, 45–46, 55–56

young athletes, 50, 51, 60, 65, 223